A SELECTION OF POEMS

BY

WILLIAM ERNEST HENLEY

Copyright © 2013 Read Books Ltd.
This book is copyright and may not be
reproduced or copied in any way without
the express permission of the publisher in writing

British Library Cataloguing-in-Publication Data
A catalogue record for this book is available from the
British Library

Contents

William Ernest Henley 1
A Child. 3
A Dainty Thing's The Villanelle. 4
A Desolate Shore 5
A Late Lark Twitters From The Quiet Skies 6
A Love By The Sea 7
A New Song to an Old Tune 8
A Thanksgiving 10
A Wink From Hesper 10
After 11
Allegro Maestoso. 12
Andante Con Moto. 15
Anterotics. 19
Apparition 20
Arabian Night's Entertainments 21
As Like The Woman As You Can. 36
At Queensferry 37
Attadale, West Highlands. 38

Ave, Caesar!	39
Back-View	40
Ballade Made In The Hot Weather	40
Ballade Of A Toyokuni Colour-Print	42
Ballade of Dead Actors	44
Ballade Of Midsummer Days And Nights	45
Ballade Of Truisms	46
Ballade Of Youth And Age	48
Barmaid	49
Before	50
Beside The Idle Summer Sea	51
Between the Dusk of a Summer Night	52
Blithe Dreams Arise To Greet Us	52
Bring Her Again, O Western Wind	55
Casualty	55
Children: Private Ward	56
Clinical	57
Croquis	59
Crosses And Troubles	60
Dedication--To My Wife	60

Discharged	61
Double Ballad Of Life And Death	62
Double Ballade on the Nothingness of Things	63
Easy is the Triolet	66
England, My England	67
Enter Patient	69
Envoy--To Charles Baxter	70
Epilogue	71
Etching	72
Fill A Glass With Golden Wine	73
Fresh From His Fastnesses	74
Friends.... Old Friends......	76
From A Window In Princes Street	77
From The Break The Nightingale	78
Grave	79
Gull In An Aery Morrice	80
Here They Trysted, And Here They Strayed	81
House-Surgeon	82
I am the Reaper	83
I Gave My Heart To A Woman	84

I. M. R. T. Hamilton Bruce (1846-1899) 85
If I Were King 86
If It Should Come To Be 86
In Fisherrow. 87
In Rotten Row. 88
In The Dials 89
In The Placid Summer Midnight 89
In The Waste Hour 91
In The Year That's Come and Gone. 93
Interior. 94
Interlude 95
Invictus. 96
It Came With The Threat Of A Waning Moon 97
Kate-A-Whimsies, John-A-Dream 98
Lady Probationer 99
Largo E Mesto 99
Last Post. 102
Let Us Be Drunk. 104
Life In Her Creaking Shoes 105
Life Is Bitter. 105

London Types:... 106

London Types: Barmaid............................... 107

London Types: Beef-Eater 108

London Types: Bluecoat Boy........................ 108

London Types: Bus Driver........................... 109

London Types: Drum-Major........................ 110

London Types: Flower-Girl 110

London Types: Hawker 111

London Types: 'Liza 112

London Types: Mounted Police 113

London Types: News Boy............................. 113

London Types: Sandwich-Man 114

London Types: The Artist Muses At His Ease 115

London Types:Life-Guardsman 115

London Voluntaries IV: Out of the Poisonous East 116

Madam Life's a Piece in Bloom 119

Margaritae Sorori 120

Midsummer Midnight Skies 121

Music 123

Nocturn 124

Not To The Staring Day 125

O Gather Me the Rose 128

O, Falmouth Is a Fine Town 129

O, Have You Blessed, Behind The Stars 131

O, Time And Change, They Range And Range 131

On The Way To Kew 132

One With The Ruined Sunset 134

Operation 134

Orientale 136

Out Of The Night That Covers Me 136

Over the Hills and Far Away 137

Pastoral 138

Praise The Generous Gods 140

Pro Rege Nostro 141

Prologue 143

Romance 144

Scherzando 145

Scrubber 148

She Saunters By The Swinging Seas 149

Some Starlit Garden Grey With Dew 149

Space And Dread and The Dark 150
Staff Nurse: New Style 152
Staff Nurse:Old Style 153
Suicide 153
The Chief. 154
The Full Sea Rolls And Thunders 155
The Gods Are Dead. 156
The Nightingale Has A Lyre Of Gold. 156
The Past Was Goodly Once 157
The Rain and the Wind 158
The Sands Are Alive With Sunshine 158
The Sea Is Full Of Wandering Foam. 159
The Shadow Of Dawn 160
The Skies Are Strown With Stars. 160
The Song Of The Sword--To Rudyard Kipling 161
The Spirit Of Wine 168
The Spring, My Dear 170
The Surges Gushed And Sounded. 170
The Wan Sun Westers, Faint And Slow. 171
The Ways Are Green 172

The Ways Of Death Are Soothing And Serene 173

The West A Glimmering Lake Of Light 174

There Is A Wheel Inside My Head 175

There's a Regret 176

Thick Is The Darkness 177

Time And The Earth 178

To Me At My Fifth-Floor Window 180

To My Mother 180

To My Wife 181

To: W A 182

Tree, Old Tree Of The Triple Crook 183

Trees And The Menace Of Night 185

Unconquerable 186

Under A Stagnant Sky 187

Vigil 189

Villanelle 191

Villon's Straight Tip to All Cross Coves 192

Visitor 193

Waiting 194

We Are The Choice Of The Will 194

We Flash Across The Level 197

We Shall Surely Die 198

We'll go No More A-Roving. 199

What Have I Done For You 200

What Is To Come 202

When The Wind Storms By With A Shout 203

When You Are Old 203

When You Wake In Your Crib 204

Where Forlorn Sunsets Flare And Fade 206

While The West Is Paling 207

Why, My Heart, Do We Love Her So? 208

You Played And Sang A Snatch Of Song 209

Your Heart Has Trembled To My Tongue 210

William Ernest Henley

William Ernest Henley was born on 23rd August 1849, in Gloucester, England.

He attended Crypt Grammar School in Gloucester where the poet, scholar, and theologian, T. E. Brown, was headmaster. Brown had a made a huge impression on the young Henley and the two struck up a lifelong friendship. Henley claimed Brown to be "a man of Genius – the first I'd ever seen", and upon Brown's death in 1897, Henley wrote an admiring obituary to him in the *New Review*.

From the age of 12, Henley suffered from tuberculosis of the bone which eventually resulted in his left leg having to be amputated below the knee. According to Robert Louis Stevenson's letters, the character of Long John Silver was inspired by his friend Henley.

In 1867, Henley passed the Oxford Local Schools Examination and set off to London to establish himself as a journalist. Unfortunately, his career was frequently interrupted by long stays in hospital due to a diseased right foot which he refused to have amputated. During a three year stay at the Royal Infirmary of Edinburgh, Henley wrote and published his collection of poetry *In Hospital* (1875). This publication is noteworthy in particular for being some of the earliest examples of free verse written in England.

Henley married Hannah (Anna) Johnson Boyle on 22nd January 1878. The couple had one daughter together, Margaret, who died at the age of five and is reportedly the source of the name Wendy in J. M. Barrie's *Peter Pan*. Apparently she used to call Barrie her "fwendy wendy", resulting in the use of the name in the children's classic.

Henley's best-remembered work is his poem "Invictus", written in 1888. It is a passionate and defiant poem, reportedly written as a demonstration of resilience following the amputation of his leg. This poem was famously recited to fellow inmates at Robben Island prison by Nelson Mandela to spread the message of empowerment and self-mastery. He also wrote a notable work of literary criticisms, *Views and Reviews,* in 1890, in which he covered a wide range of works by prominent authors.

Henley died of tuberculosis in 1903 at the age of 53 at his home in Woking, and his ashes were interred in his daughter's grave in the churchyard at Cockayne Hatley in Bedfordshire, England.

A Child

A child,
Curious and innocent,
Slips from his Nurse, and rejoicing
Loses himself in the Fair.

Thro' the jostle and din
Wandering, he revels,
Dreaming, desiring, possessing;
Till, of a sudden
Tired and afraid, he beholds
The sordid assemblage
Just as it is; and he runs
With a sob to his Nurse
(Lighting at last on him),
And in her motherly bosom
Cries him to sleep.

Thus thro' the World,
Seeing and feeling and knowing,
Goes Man: till at last,
Tired of experience, he turns
To the friendly and comforting breast
Of the old nurse, Death.

A Selection of Poems

A Dainty Thing's The Villanelle

A DAINTY thing's the Villanelle,
Sly, musical, a jewel in rhyme,
It serves its purpose passing well.

A double-clappered silver bell
That must be made to clink in chime,
A dainty thing's the Villanelle;

And if you wish to flute a spell,
Or ask a meeting 'neath the lime,
It serves its purpose passing well.

You must not ask of it the swell
Of organs grandiose and sublime--
A dainty thing's the Villanelle;

And, filled with sweetness, as a shell
Is filled with sound, and launched in time,
It serves its purpose passing well.

Still fair to see and good to smell
As in the quaintness of its prime,
A dainty thing's the Villanelle,
It serves its purpose passing well.

by William Ernest Henley

A Desolate Shore

A desolate shore,
The sinister seduction of the Moon,
The menace of the irreclaimable Sea.

Flaunting, tawdry and grim,
From cloud to cloud along her beat,
Leering her battered and inveterate leer,
She signals where he prowls in the dark alone,
Her horrible old man,
Mumbling old oaths and warming
His villainous old bones with villainous talk -
The secrets of their grisly housekeeping
Since they went out upon the pad
In the first twilight of self-conscious Time:
Growling, hideous and hoarse,
Tales of unnumbered Ships,
Goodly and strong, Companions of the Advance,
In some vile alley of the night
Waylaid and bludgeoned -
Dead.

Deep cellared in primeval ooze,
Ruined, dishonoured, spoiled,
They lie where the lean water-worm

Crawls free of their secrets, and their broken sides
Bulge with the slime of life. Thus they abide,
Thus fouled and desecrate,
The summons of the Trumpet, and the while
These Twain, their murderers,
Unravined, imperturbable, unsubdued,
Hang at the heels of their children--She aloft
As in the shining streets,
He as in ambush at some accomplice door.

The stalwart Ships,
The beautiful and bold adventurers!
Stationed out yonder in the isle,
The tall Policeman,
Flashing his bull's-eye, as he peers
About him in the ancient vacancy,
Tells them this way is safety--this way home.

A Late Lark Twitters From The Quiet Skies

the quiet skies:
And from the west,
Where the sun, his day's work ended,
Lingers as in content,
There falls on the old, gray city

by William Ernest Henley

An influence luminous and serene,
A shining peace.

The smoke ascends
In a rosy-and-golden haze. The spires
Shine and are changed. In the valley
Shadows rise. The lark sings on. The sun,
Closing his benediction,
Sinks, and the darkening air
Thrills with a sense of the triumphing night-
Night with her train of stars
And her great gift of sleep.

So be my passing!
My task accomplish'd and the long day done,
My wages taken, and in my heart
Some late lark singing,
Let me be gather'd to the quiet west,
The sundown splendid and serene,
Death.

A Love By The Sea

Out of the starless night that covers me,
(O tribulation of the wind that rolls!)

Black as the cloud of some tremendous spell,
The susurration of the sighing sea
Sounds like the sobbing whisper of two souls
That tremble in a passion of farewell.

To the desires that trebled life in me,
(O melancholy of the wind that rolls!)
The dreams that seemed the future to foretell,
The hopes that mounted herward like the sea,
To all the sweet things sent on happy souls,
I cannot choose but bid a mute farewell.

And to the girl who was so much to me
(O lamentation of this wind that rolls!)
Since I may not the life of her compel,
Out of the night, beside the sounding sea,
Full of the love that might have blent our souls,
A sad, a last, a long, supreme farewell.

A New Song to an Old Tune

SONS of Shannon, Tamar, Trent,
Men of the Lothians, Men of Kent,
Essex, Wessex, shore and shire,
Mates of the net, the mine, the fire,

by William Ernest Henley

Lads of the wheel and desk and loom,
Noble and trader, squire and groom,
Come where the bugles of England play,
'Over the hills and far away!'

Southern Cross and Polar Star --
Here are the Britons bred afar;
Serry, O serry them, fierce and keen,
Under the flag of the Empress-Queen;
Shoulder to shoulder down the track,
Where, to the unretreating Jack,
The victor bugles of England play,
'Over the hills and far away!'

What if the best of our wages be
An empty sleeve, a stiff-set knee,
A crutch for the rest of life -- who cares,
So long as the One Flag floats and dares?
So long as the One Race dares and grows?
Death -- what is death but God's own rose?
Let but the bugles of England play,
'Over the hills and far away!'

A Selection of Poems

A Thanksgiving

From brief delights that rise to me
Out of unfathomable dole,
I thank whatever gods there be
For mine unconquerable soul.
In the strong clutch of Circumstance
It has not winced, nor groaned aloud.
Before the blows of eyeless chance
My head is bloody, but unbowed.
I front unfeared the threat of space
And dwindle into dark again.
My work is done, I take my place
Among the years that wait for men.
My life, my broken life must be
One unsuccourable dole.
I thank the gods- they gave to me
A dauntless and defiant soul.

A Wink From Hesper

A wink from Hesper, falling
Fast in the wintry sky,
Comes through the even blue,
Dear, like a word from you…

by William Ernest Henley

Is it good-bye?

Across the miles between us
I send you sigh for sigh.
Good-Night, sweet friend, good-night:
Till life and all take flight,
Never good-bye.

After

Like as a flamelet blanketed in smoke,
So through the anaesthetic shows my life;
So flashes and so fades my thought, at strife
With the strong stupor that I heave and choke
And sicken at, it is so foully sweet.
Faces look strange from space-and disappear.
Far voices, sudden loud, offend my ear -
And hush as sudden. Then my senses fleet:
All were a blank, save for this dull, new pain
That grinds my leg and foot; and brokenly
Time and the place glimpse on to me again;
And, unsurprised, out of uncertainty,
I wake-relapsing-somewhat faint and fain,
To an immense, complacent dreamery.

A Selection of Poems

Allegro Maestoso

Spring winds that blow
As over leagues of myrtle-blooms and may;
Bevies of spring clouds trooping slow,
Like matrons heavy bosomed and aglow
With the mild and placid pride of increase! Nay,
What makes this insolent and comely stream
Of appetence, this freshet of desire
(Milk from the wild breasts of the wilful Day!),
Down Piccadilly dance and murmur and gleam
In genial wave on wave and gyre on gyre?
Why does that nymph unparalleled splash and churn
The wealth of her enchanted urn
Till, over-billowing all between
Her cheerful margents, grey and living green,
It floats and wanders, glittering and fleeing,
An estuary of the joy of being?
Why should the lovely leafage of the Park
Touch to an ecstasy the act of seeing?
- Sure, sure my paramour, my Bride of Brides,
Lingering and flushed, mysteriously abides
In some dim, eye-proof angle of odorous dark,
Some smiling nook of green-and-golden shade,
In the divine conviction robed and crowned
The globe fulfils his immemorial round

by William Ernest Henley

But as the marrying-place of all things made!

There is no man, this deifying day,
But feels the primal blessing in his blood.
There is no woman but disdains -
The sacred impulse of the May
Brightening like sex made sunshine through her veins -
To vail the ensigns of her womanhood.
None but, rejoicing, flaunts them as she goes,
Bounteous in looks of her delicious best,
On her inviolable quest:
These with their hopes, with their sweet secrets those,
But all desirable and frankly fair,
As each were keeping some most prosperous tryst,
And in the knowledge went imparadised!
For look! a magical influence everywhere,
Look how the liberal and transfiguring air
Washes this inn of memorable meetings,
This centre of ravishments and gracious greetings,
Till, through its jocund loveliness of length
A tidal-race of lust from shore to shore,
A brimming reach of beauty met with strength,
It shines and sounds like some miraculous dream,
Some vision multitudinous and agleam,
Of happiness as it shall be evermore!

A Selection of Poems

Praise God for giving
Through this His messenger among the days
His word the life He gave is thrice-worth living!
For Pan, the bountiful, imperious Pan -
Not dead, not dead, as impotent dreamers feigned,
But the gay genius of a million Mays
Renewing his beneficent endeavour! -
Still reigns and triumphs, as he hath triumphed and reigned
Since in the dim blue dawn of time
The universal ebb-and-flow began,
To sound his ancient music, and prevails,
By the persuasion of his mighty rhyme,
Here in this radiant and immortal street
Lavishly and omnipotently as ever
In the open hills, the undissembling dales,
The laughing-places of the juvenile earth.
For lo! the wills of man and woman meet,
Meet and are moved, each unto each endeared,
As once in Eden's prodigal bowers befell,
To share his shameless, elemental mirth
In one great act of faith: while deep and strong,
Incomparably nerved and cheered,
The enormous heart of London joys to beat
To the measures of his rough, majestic song;

by William Ernest Henley

The lewd, perennial, overmastering spell
That keeps the rolling universe ensphered,
And life, and all for which life lives to long,
Wanton and wondrous and for ever well.

Andante Con Moto

Forth from the dust and din,
The crush, the heat, the many-spotted glare,
The odour and sense of life and lust aflare,
The wrangle and jangle of unrests,
Let us take horse, Dear Heart, take horse and win -
As from swart August to the green lap of May -
To quietness and the fresh and fragrant breasts
Of the still, delicious night, not yet aware
In any of her innumerable nests
Of that first sudden plash of dawn,
Clear, sapphirine, luminous, large,
Which tells that soon the flowing springs of day
In deep and ever deeper eddies drawn
Forward and up, in wider and wider way,
Shall float the sands, and brim the shores,
On this our lith of the World, as round it roars
And spins into the outlook of the Sun
(The Lord's first gift, the Lord's especial charge),

With light, with living light, from marge to marge
Until the course He set and staked be run.

Through street and square, through square and street,
Each with his home-grown quality of dark
And violated silence, loud and fleet,
Waylaid by a merry ghost at every lamp,
The hansom wheels and plunges. Hark, O, hark,
Sweet, how the old mare's bit and chain
Ring back a rough refrain
Upon the marked and cheerful tramp
Of her four shoes! Here is the Park,
And O, the languid midsummer wafts adust,
The tired midsummer blooms!
O, the mysterious distances, the glooms
Romantic, the august
And solemn shapes! At night this City of Trees
Turns to a tryst of vague and strange
And monstrous Majesties,
Let loose from some dim underworld to range
These terrene vistas till their twilight sets:
When, dispossessed of wonderfulness, they stand
Beggared and common, plain to all the land
For stooks of leaves! And lo! the Wizard Hour,
His silent, shining sorcery winged with power!
Still, still the streets, between their carcanets

by William Ernest Henley

Of linking gold, are avenues of sleep.
But see how gable ends and parapets
In gradual beauty and significance
Emerge! And did you hear
That little twitter-and-cheep,
Breaking inordinately loud and clear
On this still, spectral, exquisite atmosphere?
'Tis a first nest at matins! And behold
A rakehell cat--how furtive and acold!
A spent witch homing from some infamous dance -
Obscene, quick-trotting, see her tip and fade
Through shadowy railings into a pit of shade!
And now! a little wind and shy,
The smell of ships (that earnest of romance),
A sense of space and water, and thereby
A lamplit bridge ouching the troubled sky,
And look, O, look! a tangle of silver gleams
And dusky lights, our River and all his dreams,
His dreams that never save in our deaths can die.

What miracle is happening in the air,
Charging the very texture of the gray
With something luminous and rare?
The night goes out like an ill-parcelled fire,
And, as one lights a candle, it is day.
The extinguisher, that perks it like a spire

A Selection of Poems

On the little formal church, is not yet green
Across the water: but the house-tops nigher,
The corner-lines, the chimneys--look how clean,
How new, how naked! See the batch of boats,
Here at the stairs, washed in the fresh-sprung beam!
And those are barges that were goblin floats,
Black, hag-steered, fraught with devilry and dream!
And in the piles the water frolics clear,
The ripples into loose rings wander and flee,
And we--we can behold that could but hear
The ancient River singing as he goes,
New-mailed in morning, to the ancient Sea.
The gas burns lank and jaded in its glass:
The old Ruffian soon shall yawn himself awake,
And light his pipe, and shoulder his tools, and take
His hobnailed way to work!

Let us too pass -
Pass ere the sun leaps and your shadow shows -
Through these long, blindfold rows
Of casements staring blind to right and left,
Each with his gaze turned inward on some piece
Of life in death's own likeness--Life bereft
Of living looks as by the Great Release -
Pass to an exquisite night's more exquisite close!

by William Ernest Henley

Reach upon reach of burial--so they feel,
These colonies of dreams! And as we steal
Homeward together, but for the buxom breeze,
Fitfully frolicking to heel
With news of dawn-drenched woods and tumbling seas,
We might--thus awed, thus lonely that we are -
Be wandering some dispeopled star,
Some world of memories and unbroken graves,
So broods the abounding Silence near and far:
Till even your footfall craves
Forgiveness of the majesty it braves.

Anterotics

Laughs the happy April morn
Thro' my grimy, little window,
And a shaft of sunshine pushes
Thro' the shadows in the square.

Dogs are tracing thro' the grass,
Crows are cawing round the chimneys,
In and out among the washing
Goes the West at hide-and-seek.

Loud and cheerful clangs the bell.
Here the nurses troop to breakfast.
Handsome, ugly, all are women . . .
O, the Spring--the Spring--the Spring!

Apparition

Thin-legged, thin-chested, slight unspeakably,
Neat-footed and weak-fingered: in his face -
Lean, large-boned, curved of beak, and touched with race,
Bold-lipped, rich-tinted, mutable as the sea,
The brown eyes radiant with vivacity -
There shines a brilliant and romantic grace,
A spirit intense and rare, with trace on trace
Of passion and impudence and energy.
Valiant in velvet, light in ragged luck,
Most vain, most generous, sternly critical,
Buffoon and poet, lover and sensualist:
A deal of Ariel, just a streak of Puck,
Much Antony, of Hamlet most of all,
And something of the Shorter-Catechist.

by William Ernest Henley

Arabian Night's Entertainments

Once on a time
There was a little boy: a master-mage
By virtue of a Book
Of magic--O, so magical it filled
His life with visionary pomps
Processional! And Powers
Passed with him where he passed. And Thrones
And Dominations, glaived and plumed and mailed,
Thronged in the criss-cross streets,
The palaces pell-mell with playing-fields,
Domes, cloisters, dungeons, caverns, tents, arcades,
Of the unseen, silent City, in his soul
Pavilioned jealously, and hid
As in the dusk, profound,
Green stillnesses of some enchanted mere. -

I shut mine eyes . . . And lo!
A flickering snatch of memory that floats
Upon the face of a pool of darkness five
And thirty dead years deep,
Antic in girlish broideries
And skirts and silly shoes with straps
And a broad-ribanded leghorn, he walks
Plain in the shadow of a church

A Selection of Poems

(St. Michael's: in whose brazen call
To curfew his first wails of wrath were whelmed),
Sedate for all his haste
To be at home; and, nestled in his arm,
Inciting still to quiet and solitude,
Boarded in sober drab,
With small, square, agitating cuts
Let in a-top of the double-columned, close,
Quakerlike print, a Book! . . .
What but that blessed brief
Of what is gallantest and best
In all the full-shelved Libraries of Romance?
The Book of rocs,
Sandalwood, ivory, turbans, ambergris,
Cream-tarts, and lettered apes, and calendars,
And ghouls, and genies--O, so huge
They might have overed the tall Minster Tower
Hands down, as schoolboys take a post!
In truth, the Book of Camaralzaman,
Schemselnihar and Sindbad, Scheherezade
The peerless, Bedreddin, Badroulbadour,
Cairo and Serendib and Candahar,
And Caspian, and the dim, terrific bulk -
Ice-ribbed, fiend-visited, isled in spells and storms -
Of Kaf! . . . That centre of miracles,
The sole, unparalleled Arabian Nights!

by William Ernest Henley

Old friends I had a-many--kindly and grim
Familiars, cronies quaint
And goblin! Never a Wood but housed
Some morrice of dainty dapperlings. No Brook
But had his nunnery
Of green-haired, silvry-curving sprites,
To cabin in his grots, and pace
His lilied margents. Every lone Hillside
Might open upon Elf-Land. Every Stalk
That curled about a Bean-stick was of the breed
Of that live ladder by whose delicate rungs
You climbed beyond the clouds, and found
The Farm-House where the Ogre, gorged
And drowsy, from his great oak chair,
Among the flitches and pewters at the fire,
Called for his Faery Harp. And in it flew,
And, perching on the kitchen table, sang
Jocund and jubilant, with a sound
Of those gay, golden-vowered madrigals
The shy thrush at mid-May
Flutes from wet orchards flushed with the triumphing dawn;
Or blackbirds rioting as they listened still,
In old-world woodlands rapt with an old-world spring,

For Pan's own whistle, savage and rich and lewd,
And mocked him call for call!

I could not pass
The half-door where the cobbler sat in view
Nor figure me the wizen Leprechaun,
In square-cut, faded reds and buckle-shoes,
Bent at his work in the hedge-side, and know
Just how he tapped his brogue, and twitched
His wax-end this and that way, both with wrists
And elbows. In the rich June fields,
Where the ripe clover drew the bees,
And the tall quakers trembled, and the West Wind
Lolled his half-holiday away
Beside me lolling and lounging through my own,
'Twas good to follow the Miller's Youngest Son
On his white horse along the leafy lanes;
For at his stirrup linked and ran,
Not cynical and trapesing, as he loped
From wall to wall above the espaliers,
But in the bravest tops
That market-town, a town of tops, could show:
Bold, subtle, adventurous, his tail
A banner flaunted in disdain
Of human stratagems and shifts:
King over All the Catlands, present and past

by William Ernest Henley

And future, that moustached
Artificer of fortunes, Puss-in-Boots!
Or Bluebeard's Closet, with its plenishing
Of meat-hooks, sawdust, blood,
And wives that hung like fresh-dressed carcases -
Odd-fangled, most a butcher's, part
A faery chamber hazily seen
And hazily figured--on dark afternoons
And windy nights was visiting of the best.
Then, too, the pelt of hoofs
Out in the roaring darkness told
Of Herne the Hunter in his antlered helm
Galloping, as with despatches from the Pit,
Between his hell-born Hounds.
And Rip Van Winkle . . . often I lurked to hear,
Outside the long, low timbered, tarry wall,
The mutter and rumble of the trolling bowls
Down the lean plank, before they fluttered the pins;
For, listening, I could help him play
His wonderful game,
In those blue, booming hills, with Mariners
Refreshed from kegs not coopered in this our world.

But what were these so near,
So neighbourly fancies to the spell that brought
The run of Ali Baba's Cave

A Selection of Poems

Just for the saying 'Open Sesame,'
With gold to measure, peck by peck,
In round, brown wooden stoups
You borrowed at the chandler's? . . . Or one time
Made you Aladdin's friend at school,
Free of his Garden of Jewels, Ring and Lamp
In perfect trim? . . . Or Ladies, fair
For all the embrowning scars in their white breasts
Went labouring under some dread ordinance,
Which made them whip, and bitterly cry the while,
Strange Curs that cried as they,
Till there was never a Black Bitch of all
Your consorting but might have gone
Spell-driven miserably for crimes
Done in the pride of womanhood and desire . . .
Or at the ghostliest altitudes of night,
While you lay wondering and acold,
Your sense was fearfully purged; and soon
Queen Labe, abominable and dear,
Rose from your side, opened the Box of Doom,
Scattered the yellow powder (which I saw
Like sulphur at the Docks in bulk),
And muttered certain words you could not hear;
And there! a living stream,
The brook you bathed in, with its weeds and flags
And cresses, glittered and sang

by William Ernest Henley

Out of the hearthrug over the nakedness,
Fair-scrubbed and decent, of your bedroom floor! . . .

I was--how many a time! -
That Second Calendar, Son of a King,
On whom 'twas vehemently enjoined,
Pausing at one mysterious door,
To pry no closer, but content his soul
With his kind Forty. Yet I could not rest
For idleness and ungovernable Fate.
And the Black Horse, which fed on sesame
(That wonder-working word!),
Vouchsafed his back to me, and spread his vans,
And soaring, soaring on
From air to air, came charging to the ground
Sheer, like a lark from the midsummer clouds,
And, shaking me out of the saddle, where I sprawled
Flicked at me with his tail,
And left me blinded, miserable, distraught
(Even as I was in deed,
When doctors came, and odious things were done
On my poor tortured eyes
With lancets; or some evil acid stung
And wrung them like hot sand,
And desperately from room to room
Fumble I must my dark, disconsolate way),

A Selection of Poems

To get to Bagdad how I might. But there
I met with Merry Ladies. O you three -
Safie, Amine, Zobeide--when my heart
Forgets you all shall be forgot!
And so we supped, we and the rest,
On wine and roasted lamb, rose-water, dates,
Almonds, pistachios, citrons. And Haroun
Laughed out of his lordly beard
On Giaffar and Mesrour (I knew the Three
For all their Mossoul habits). And outside
The Tigris, flowing swift
Like Severn bend for bend, twinkled and gleamed
With broken and wavering shapes of stranger stars;
The vast, blue night
Was murmurous with peris' plumes
And the leathern wings of genies; words of power
Were whispering; and old fishermen,
Casting their nets with prayer, might draw to shore
Dead loveliness: or a prodigy in scales
Worth in the Caliph's Kitchen pieces of gold:
Or copper vessels, stopped with lead,
Wherein some Squire of Eblis watched and railed,
In durance under potent charactry
Graven by the seal of Solomon the King . . .

Then, as the Book was glassed

by William Ernest Henley

In Life as in some olden mirror's quaint,
Bewildering angles, so would Life
Flash light on light back on the Book; and both
Were changed. Once in a house decayed
From better days, harbouring an errant show
(For all its stories of dry-rot
Were filled with gruesome visitants in wax,
Inhuman, hushed, ghastly with Painted Eyes),
I wandered; and no living soul
Was nearer than the pay-box; and I stared
Upon them staring--staring. Till at last,
Three sets of rafters from the streets,
I strayed upon a mildewed, rat-run room,
With the two Dancers, horrible and obscene,
Guarding the door: and there, in a bedroom-set,
Behind a fence of faded crimson cords,
With an aspect of frills
And dimities and dishonoured privacy
That made you hanker and hesitate to look,
A Woman with her litter of Babes--all slain,
All in their nightgowns, all with Painted Eyes
Staring--still staring; so that I turned and ran
As for my neck, but in the street
Took breath. The same, it seemed,
And yet not all the same, I was to find,
As I went up! For afterwards,

A Selection of Poems

Whenas I went my round alone -
All day alone--in long, stern, silent streets,
Where I might stretch my hand and take
Whatever I would: still there were Shapes of Stone,
Motionless, lifelike, frightening--for the Wrath
Had smitten them; but they watched,
This by her melons and figs, that by his rings
And chains and watches, with the hideous gaze,
The Painted Eyes insufferable,
Now, of those grisly images; and I
Pursued my best-beloved quest,
Thrilled with a novel and delicious fear.
So the night fell--with never a lamplighter;
And through the Palace of the King
I groped among the echoes, and I felt
That they were there,
Dreadfully there, the Painted staring Eyes,
Hall after hall . . . Till lo! from far
A Voice! And in a little while
Two tapers burning! And the Voice,
Heard in the wondrous Word of God, was--whose?
Whose but Zobeide's,
The lady of my heart, like me
A True Believer, and like me
An outcast thousands of leagues beyond the pale! . . .

by William Ernest Henley

Or, sailing to the Isles
Of Khaledan, I spied one evenfall
A black blotch in the sunset; and it grew
Swiftly . . . and grew. Tearing their beards,
The sailors wept and prayed; but the grave ship,
Deep laden with spiceries and pearls, went mad,
Wrenched the long tiller out of the steersman's hand,
And, turning broadside on,
As the most iron would, was haled and sucked
Nearer, and nearer yet;
And, all awash, with horrible lurching leaps
Rushed at that Portent, casting a shadow now
That swallowed sea and sky; and then,
Anchors and nails and bolts
Flew screaming out of her, and with clang on clang,
A noise of fifty stithies, caught at the sides
Of the Magnetic Mountain; and she lay,
A broken bundle of firewood, strown piecemeal
About the waters; and her crew
Passed shrieking, one by one; and I was left
To drown. All the long night I swam;
But in the morning, O, the smiling coast
Tufted with date-trees, meadowlike,
Skirted with shelving sands! And a great wave
Cast me ashore; and I was saved alive.
So, giving thanks to God, I dried my clothes,

And, faring inland, in a desert place
I stumbled on an iron ring -
The fellow of fifty built into the Quays:
When, scenting a trap-door,
I dug, and dug; until my biggest blade
Stuck into wood. And then,
The flight of smooth-hewn, easy-falling stairs,
Sunk in the naked rock! The cool, clean vault,
So neat with niche on niche it might have been
Our beer-cellar but for the rows
Of brazen urns (like monstrous chemist's jars)
Full to the wide, squat throats
With gold-dust, but a-top
A layer of pickled-walnut-looking things
I knew for olives! And far, O, far away,
The Princess of China languished! Far away
Was marriage, with a Vizier and a Chief
Of Eunuchs and the privilege
Of going out at night
To play--unkenned, majestical, secure -
Where the old, brown, friendly river shaped
Like Tigris shore for shore! Haply a Ghoul
Sat in the churchyard under a frightened moon,
A thighbone in his fist, and glared
At supper with a Lady: she who took
Her rice with tweezers grain by grain.

by William Ernest Henley

Or you might stumble--there by the iron gates
Of the Pump Room--underneath the limes -
Upon Bedreddin in his shirt and drawers,
Just as the civil Genie laid him down.
Or those red-curtained panes,
Whence a tame cornet tenored it throatily
Of beer-pots and spittoons and new long pipes,
Might turn a caravansery's, wherein
You found Noureddin Ali, loftily drunk,
And that fair Persian, bathed in tears,
You'd not have given away
For all the diamonds in the Vale Perilous
You had that dark and disleaved afternoon
Escaped on a roc's claw,
Disguised like Sindbad--but in Christmas beef!
And all the blissful while
The schoolboy satchel at your hip
Was such a bulse of gems as should amaze
Grey-whiskered chapmen drawn
From over Caspian: yea, the Chief Jewellers
Of Tartary and the bazaars,
Seething with traffic, of enormous Ind. -

Thus cried, thus called aloud, to the child heart
The magian East: thus the child eyes
Spelled out the wizard message by the light

Of the sober, workaday hours
They saw, week in week out, pass, and still pass
In the sleepy Minster City, folded kind
In ancient Severn's arm,
Amongst her water-meadows and her docks,
Whose floating populace of ships -
Galliots and luggers, light-heeled brigantines,
Bluff barques and rake-hell fore-and-afters--brought
To her very doorsteps and geraniums
The scents of the World's End; the calls
That may not be gainsaid to rise and ride
Like fire on some high errand of the race;
The irresistible appeals
For comradeship that sound
Steadily from the irresistible sea.
Thus the East laughed and whispered, and the tale,
Telling itself anew
In terms of living, labouring life,
Took on the colours, busked it in the wear
Of life that lived and laboured; and Romance,
The Angel-Playmate, raining down
His golden influences
On all I saw, and all I dreamed and did,
Walked with me arm in arm,
Or left me, as one bediademed with straws
And bits of glass, to gladden at my heart

by William Ernest Henley

Who had the gift to seek and feel and find
His fiery-hearted presence everywhere.
Even so dear Hesper, bringer of all good things,
Sends the same silver dews
Of happiness down her dim, delighted skies
On some poor collier-hamlet--(mound on mound
Of sifted squalor; here a soot-throated stalk
Sullenly smoking over a row
Of flat-faced hovels; black in the gritty air
A web of rails and wheels and beams; with strings
Of hurtling, tipping trams) -
As on the amorous nightingales
And roses of Shiraz, or the walls and towers
Of Samarcand--the Ineffable--whence you espy
The splendour of Ginnistan's embattled spears,
Like listed lightnings.
Samarcand!
That name of names! That star-vaned belvedere
Builded against the Chambers of the South!
That outpost on the Infinite!
And behold!
Questing therefrom, you knew not what wild tide
Might overtake you: for one fringe,
One suburb, is stablished on firm earth; but one
Floats founded vague
In lubberlands delectable--isles of palm

And lotus, fortunate mains, far-shimmering seas,
The promise of wistful hills -
The shining, shifting Sovranties of Dream.

As Like The Woman As You Can

'As like the Woman as you can' -
(Thus the New Adam was beguiled) -
'So shall you touch the Perfect Man' -
(God in the Garden heard and smiled).
'Your father perished with his day:
'A clot of passions fierce and blind,
'He fought, he hacked, he crushed his way:
'Your muscles, Child, must be of mind.

'The Brute that lurks and irks within,
'How, till you have him gagged and bound,
'Escape the foullest form of Sin?'
(God in the Garden laughed and frowned).
'So vile, so rank, the bestial mood
'In which the race is bid to be,
'It wrecks the Rarer Womanhood:
'Live, therefore, you, for Purity!

'Take for your mate no gallant croup,

by William Ernest Henley

'No girl all grace and natural will:
'To work her mission were to stoop,
'Maybe to lapse, from Well to Ill.
'Choose one of whom your grosser make' -
(God in the Garden laughed outright) -
'The true refining touch may take,
'Till both attain to Life's last height.

'There, equal, purged of soul and sense.
'Beneficent, high-thinking, just,
'Beyond the appeal of Violence,
'Incapable of common Lust,
'In mental Marriage still prevail' -
(God in the Garden hid His face) -
'Till you achieve that Female-Male
'In Which shall culminate the race.'

At Queensferry

The blackbird sang, the skies were clear and clean
We bowled along a road that curved a spine
Superbly sinuous and serpentine
Thro' silent symphonies of summer green.
Sudden the Forth came on us--sad of mien,
No cloud to colour it, no breeze to line:

A sheet of dark, dull glass, without a sign
Of life or death, two spits of sand between.
Water and sky merged blank in mist together,
The Fort loomed spectral, and the Guardship's spars
Traced vague, black shadows on the shimmery glaze:
We felt the dim, strange years, the grey, strange weather,
The still, strange land, unvexed of sun or stars,
Where Lancelot rides clanking thro' the haze.

Attadale, West Highlands

A black and glassy float, opaque and still,
The loch, at furthest ebb supine in sleep,
Reversing, mirrored in its luminous deep
The calm grey skies; the solemn spurs of hill;
Heather, and corn, and wisps of loitering haze;
The wee white cots, black-hatted, plumed with smoke;
The braes beyond--and when the ripple awoke,
They wavered with the jarred and wavering glaze.
The air was hushed and dreamy. Evermore
A noise of running water whispered near.
A straggling crow called high and thin. A bird
Trilled from the birch-leaves. Round the shingled shore,

by William Ernest Henley

Yellow with weed, there wandered, vague and clear,
Strange vowels, mysterious gutturals, idly heard.

Ave, Caesar!

From the winter's grey despair,
From the summer's golden languor,
Death, the lover of Life,
Frees us for ever.

Inevitable, silent, unseen,
Everywhere always,
Shadow by night and as light in the day,
Signs she at last to her chosen;
And, as she waves them forth,
Sorrow and Joy
Lay by their looks and their voices,
Set down their hopes, and are made
One in the dim Forever.

Into the winter's grey delight,
Into the summer's golden dream,
Holy and high and impartial,
Death, the mother of Life,
Mingles all men for ever.

A Selection of Poems

Back-View

I watched you saunter down the sand:
Serene and large, the golden weather
Flowed radiant round your peacock feather,
And glistered from your jewelled hand.
Your tawny hair, turned strand on strand
And bound with blue ribands together,
Streaked the rough tartan, green like heather,
That round your lissome shoulder spanned.
Your grace was quick my sense to seize:
The quaint looped hat, the twisted tresses,
The close-drawn scarf, and under these
The flowing, flapping draperies -
My thought an outline still caresses,
Enchanting, comic, Japanese!

Ballade Made In The Hot Weather

Fountains that frisk and sprinkle
The moss they overspill;
Pools that the breezes crinkle;
The wheel beside the mill,
With its wet, weedy frill;
Wind-shadows in the wheat;

by William Ernest Henley

A water-cart in the street;
The fringe of foam that girds
An islet's ferneries;
A green sky's minor thirds -
To live, I think of these!

Of ice and glass the tinkle,
Pellucid, silver-shrill;
Peaches without a wrinkle;
Cherries and snow at will,
From china bowls that fill
The senses with a sweet
Incuriousness of heat;
A melon's dripping sherds;
Cream-clotted strawberries;
Dusk dairies set with curds -
To live, I think of these!

Vale-lily and periwinkle;
Wet stone-crop on the sill;
The look of leaves a-twinkle
With windlets clear and still;
The feel of a forest rill
That wimples fresh and fleet
About one's naked feet;
The muzzles of drinking herds;

Lush flags and bulrushes;
The chirp of rain-bound birds -
To live, I think of these!

Envoy

Dark aisles, new packs of cards,
Mermaidens' tails, cool swards,
Dawn dews and starlit seas,
White marbles, whiter words -
To live, I think of these!

Ballade Of A Toyokuni Colour-Print

Was I a Samurai renowned,
Two-sworded, fierce, immense of bow?
A histrion angular and profound?
A priest? a porter?--Child, although
I have forgotten clean, I know
That in the shade of Fujisan,
What time the cherry-orchards blow,
I loved you once in old Japan.

As here you loiter, flowing-gowned
And hugely sashed, with pins a-row

by William Ernest Henley

Your quaint head as with flamelets crowned,
Demure, inviting--even so,
When merry maids in Miyako
To feel the sweet o' the year began,
And green gardens to overflow,
I loved you once in old Japan.

Clear shine the hills; the rice-fields round
Two cranes are circling; sleepy and slow,
A blue canal the lake's blue bound
Breaks at the bamboo bridge; and lo!
Touched with the sundown's spirit and glow,
I see you turn, with flirted fan,
Against the plum-tree's bloomy snow . . .
I loved you once in old Japan!

Envoy

Dear, 'twas a dozen lives ago;
But that I was a lucky man
The Toyokuni here will show:
I loved you--once--in old Japan.

A Selection of Poems

Ballade of Dead Actors

Where are the passions they essayed,
And where the tears they made to flow?
Where the wild humours they portrayed
For laughing worlds to see and know?
Othello's wrath and Juliet's woe?
Sir Peter's whims and Timon's gall?
And Millamant and Romeo?
Into the night go one and all.
Where are the braveries, fresh or frayed?
The plumes, the armours -- friend and foe?
The cloth of gold, the rare brocade,
The mantles glittering to and fro?
The pomp, the pride, the royal show?
The cries of war and festival?
The youth, the grace, the charm, the glow?
Into the night go one and all.
The curtain falls, the play is played:
The Beggar packs beside the Beau;
The Monarch troops, and troops the Maid;
The Thunder huddles with the Snow.
Where are the revellers high and low?
The clashing swords? The lover's call?
The dancers gleaming row on row?
Into the night go one and all.

by William Ernest Henley

Ballade Of Midsummer Days And Nights

With a ripple of leaves and a tinkle of streams
The full world rolls in a rhythm of praise,
And the winds are one with the clouds and beams -
Midsummer days! Midsummer days!
The dusk grows vast; in a purple haze,
While the West from a rapture of sunset rights,
Faint stars their exquisite lamps upraise -
Midsummer nights! O midsummer nights!

The wood's green heart is a nest of dreams,
The lush grass thickens and springs and sways,
The rathe wheat rustles, the landscape gleams -
Midsummer days! Midsummer days!
In the stilly fields, in the stilly ways,
All secret shadows and mystic lights,
Late lovers murmur and linger and gaze -
Midsummer nights! O midsummer nights!

There's a music of bells from the trampling teams,
Wild skylarks hover, the gorses blaze,
The rich, ripe rose as with incense steams -
Midsummer days! Midsummer days!
A soul from the honeysuckle strays,
And the nightingale as from prophet heights

Sings to the Earth of her million Mays -
Midsummer nights! O midsummer nights!

Envoy

And it's O, for my dear and the charm that stays -
Midsummer days! Midsummer days!
It's O, for my Love and the dark that plights -
Midsummer nights! O midsummer nights!

Ballade Of Truisms

Gold or silver, every day,
Dies to gray.
There are knots in every skein.
Hours of work and hours of play
Fade away
Into one immense Inane.
Shadow and substance, chaff and grain,
Are as vain
As the foam or as the spray.
Life goes crooning, faint and fain,
One refrain:
'If it could be always May!'

by William Ernest Henley

Though the earth be green and gay,
Though, they say,
Man the cup of heaven may drain;
Though, his little world to sway,
He display
Hoard on hoard of pith and brain:
Autumn brings a mist and rain
That constrain

Him and his to know decay,
Where undimmed the lights that wane
Would remain,
If it could be always May.

YEA, alas, must turn to NAY,
Flesh to clay.
Chance and Time are ever twain.
Men may scoff, and men may pray,
But they pay
Every pleasure with a pain.
Life may soar, and Fortune deign
To explain
Where her prizes hide and stay;
But we lack the lusty train
We should gain,
If it could be always May.

Envoy

Time, the pedagogue, his cane
Might retain,
But his charges all would stray
Truanting in every lane -
Jack with Jane -
If it could be always May.

Ballade Of Youth And Age

Spring at her height on a morn at prime,
Sails that laugh from a flying squall,
Pomp of harmony, rapture of rhyme -
Youth is the sign of them, one and all.
Winter sunsets and leaves that fall,
An empty flagon, a folded page,
A tumble-down wheel, a tattered ball -
These are a type of the world of Age.

Bells that clash in a gaudy chime,
Swords that clatter in onsets tall,
The words that ring and the fames that climb -
Youth is the sign of them, one and all.

by William Ernest Henley

Hymnals old in a dusty stall,
A bald, blind bird in a crazy cage,
The scene of a faded festival -
These are a type of the world of Age.

Hours that strut as the heirs of time,
Deeds whose rumour's a clarion-call,
Songs where the singers their souls sublime -
Youth is the sign of them, one and all.
A staff that rests in a nook of wall,
A reeling battle, a rusted gage,
The chant of a nearing funeral -
These are a type of the world of Age.

Envoy

Struggle and turmoil, revel and brawl -
Youth is the sign of them, one and all.
A smouldering hearth and a silent stage -
These are a type of the world of Age.

Barmaid

Though, if you ask her name, she says Elise,
Being plain Elizabeth, e'en let it pass,

And own that, if her aspirates take their ease,
She ever makes a point, in washing glass,
Handling the engine, turning taps for tots,
And countering change, and scorning what men say,
Of posing as a dove among the pots,
Nor often gives her dignity away.
Her head's a work of art, and, if her eyes
Be tired and ignorant, she has a waist;
Cheaply the Mode she shadows; and she tries
From penny novels to amend her taste;
And, having mopped the zinc for certain years,
And faced the gas, she fades and disappears.

Before

Behold me waiting-waiting for the knife.
A little while, and at a leap I storm
The thick, sweet mystery of chloroform,
The drunken dark, the little death-in-life.
The gods are good to me: I have no wife,
No innocent child, to think of as I near
The fateful minute; nothing all-too dear
Unmans me for my bout of passive strife.
Yet am I tremulous and a trifle sick,
And, face to face with chance, I shrink a little:

by William Ernest Henley

My hopes are strong, my will is something weak.
Here comes the basket? Thank you. I am ready.
But, gentlemen my porters, life is brittle:
You carry Caesar and his fortunes-steady!

Beside The Idle Summer Sea

Beside the idle summer sea,
And in the vacant summer days,
Light Love came fluting down the ways,
Where you were loitering with me.

Who have not welcomed even as we,
That jocund minstrel and his lays
Beside the idle summer sea
And in the vacant summer days?

We listened, we were fancy-free;
And lo! in terror and amaze
We stood alone – alone and gaze
With an implacable memory
Beside the idle summer sea.

A Selection of Poems

Between the Dusk of a Summer Night

Between the dusk of a summer night
And the dawn of a summer day,
We caught at a mood as it passed in flight,
And we bade it stoop and stay.
And what with the dawn of night began
With the dusk of day was done;
For that is the way of woman and man,
When a hazard has made them one.
Arc upon arc, from shade to shine,
The World went thundering free;
And what was his errand but hers and mine --
The lords of him, I and she?
O, it's die we must, but it's live we can,
And the marvel of earth and sun
Is all for the joy of woman and man
And the longing that makes them one.

Blithe Dreams Arise To Greet Us

Blithe dreams arise to greet us,
And life feels clean and new,
For the old love comes to meet us
In the dawning and the dew.

by William Ernest Henley

O'erblown with sunny shadows,
O'ersped with winds at play,
The woodlands and the meadows
Are keeping holiday.
Wild foals are scampering, neighing,
Brave merles their hautboys blow:
Come! let us go a-maying
As in the Long-Ago.

Here we but peak and dwindle:
The clank of chain and crane,
The whir of crank and spindle
Bewilder heart and brain;
The ends of our endeavour
Are merely wealth and fame,
Yet in the still Forever
We're one and all the same;
Delaying, still delaying,
We watch the fading west:
Come! let us go a-maying,
Nor fear to take the best.

Yet beautiful and spacious
The wise, old world appears.
Yet frank and fair and gracious
Outlaugh the jocund years.

A Selection of Poems

Our arguments disputing,
The universal Pan
Still wanders fluting--fluting -
Fluting to maid and man.
Our weary well-a-waying
His music cannot still:
Come! let us go a-maying,
And pipe with him our fill.

When wanton winds are flowing
Among the gladdening glass;
Where hawthorn brakes are blowing,
And meadow perfumes pass;
Where morning's grace is greenest,
And fullest noon's of pride;
Where sunset spreads serenest,
And sacred night's most wide;
Where nests are swaying, swaying,
And spring's fresh voices call,
Come! let us go a-maying,
And bless the God of all!

by William Ernest Henley

Bring Her Again, O Western Wind

Bring her again, O western wind,
Over the western sea!
Gentle and good and fair and kind,
Bring her again to me!

Not that her fancy holds me dear,
Not that a hope may be:
Only that I may know her near,
Wind of the western sea!

Casualty

As with varnish red and glistening
Dripped his hair; his feet looked rigid;
Raised, he settled stiffly sideways:
You could see his hurts were spinal.

He had fallen from an engine,
And been dragged along the metals.
It was hopeless, and they knew it;
So they covered him, and left him.

As he lay, by fits half sentient,

Inarticulately moaning,
With his stockinged soles protruded
Stark and awkward from the blankets,

To his bed there came a woman,
Stood and looked and sighed a little,
And departed without speaking,
As himself a few hours after.

I was told it was his sweetheart.
They were on the eve of marriage.
She was quiet as a statue,
But her lip was grey and writhen.

Children: Private Ward

Here in this dim, dull, double-bedded room,
I play the father to a brace of boys,
Ailing but apt for every sort of noise,
Bedfast but brilliant yet with health and bloom.
Roden, the Irishman, is 'sieven past,'
Blue-eyed, snub-nosed, chubby, and fair of face.
Willie's but six, and seems to like the place,
A cheerful little collier to the last.
They eat, and laugh, and sing, and fight, all day;

by William Ernest Henley

All night they sleep like dormice. See them play
At Operations:- Roden, the Professor,
Saws, lectures, takes the artery up, and ties;
Willie, self-chloroformed, with half-shut eyes,
Holding the limb and moaning-Case and Dresser.

Clinical

Hist? . . .
Through the corridor's echoes,
Louder and nearer
Comes a great shuffling of feet.
Quick, every one of you,
Strighten your quilts, and be decent!
Here's the Professor.

In he comes first
With the bright look we know,
From the broad, white brows the kind eyes
Soothing yet nerving you. Here at his elbow,
White-capped, white-aproned, the Nurse,
Towel on arm and her inkstand
Fretful with quills.
Here in the ruck, anyhow,
Surging along,

A Selection of Poems

Louts, duffers, exquisites, students, and prigs -
Whiskers and foreheads, scarf-pins and spectacles -
Hustles the Class! And they ring themselves
Round the first bed, where the Chief
(His dressers and clerks at attention),
Bends in inspection already.

So shows the ring
Seen from behind round a conjurer
Doing his pitch in the street.
High shoulders, low shoulders, broad shoulders, narrow ones,
Round, square, and angular, serry and shove;
While from within a voice,
Gravely and weightily fluent,
Sounds; and then ceases; and suddenly
(Look at the stress of the shoulders!)
Out of a quiver of silence,
Over the hiss of the spray,
Comes a low cry, and the sound
Of breath quick intaken through teeth
Clenched in resolve. And the Master
Breaks from the crowd, and goes,
Wiping his hands,
To the next bed, with his pupils
Flocking and whispering behind him.

by William Ernest Henley

Now one can see.
Case Number One
Sits (rather pale) with his bedclothes
Stripped up, and showing his foot
(Alas for God's Image!)
Swaddled in wet, white lint
Brilliantly hideous with red.

Croquis

The beach was crowded. Pausing now and then,
He groped and fiddled doggedly along,
His worn face glaring on the thoughtless throng
The stony peevishness of sightless men.
He seemed scarce older than his clothes. Again,
Grotesquing thinly many an old sweet song,
So cracked his fiddle, his hand so frail and wrong,
You hardly could distinguish one in ten.
He stopped at last, and sat him on the sand,
And, grasping wearily his bread-winner,
Staring dim towards the blue immensity,
Then leaned his head upon his poor old hand.
He may have slept: he did not speak nor stir:
His gesture spoke a vast despondency.

A Selection of Poems

Crosses And Troubles

Crosses and troubles a-many have proved me.
One or two women (God bless them) have loved me.
I have worked and dreamed, and I've talked at will.
Of art and drink I have had my fill.
I've comforted here, and I succoured there.
I've faced my foes, and I backed my friends.
I've blundered, and sometimes made amends.
I've prayed for light, and I've known despair.
Now I look before, as I look behind,
Come storm, come shine, whatever befall,
With a grateful heart and a constant mind,
For the end I know is the best of all.

Dedication--To My Wife

Take, dear, my little sheaf of songs,
For, old or new,
All that is good in them belongs
Only to you;

And, singing as when all was young,
They will recall

by William Ernest Henley

Those others, lived but left unsung -
The bent of all.

Discharged

Carry me out
Into the wind and the sunshine,
Into the beautiful world.

O, the wonder, the spell of the streets!
The stature and strength of the horses,
The rustle and echo of footfalls,
The flat roar and rattle of wheels!
A swift tram floats huge on us . . .
It's a dream?
The smell of the mud in my nostrils
Blows brave-like a breath of the sea!

As of old,
Ambulant, undulant drapery,
Vaguery and strangely provocative,
Fluttersd and beckons. O, yonder -
Is it?-the gleam of a stocking!
Sudden, a spire
Wedged in the mist! O, the houses,

The long lines of lofty, grey houses,
Cross-hatched with shadow and light!
These are the streets . . .
Each is an avenue leading
Whither I will!

Free . . . !
Dizzy, hysterical, faint,
I sit, and the carriage rolls on with me
Into the wonderful world.

Double Ballad Of Life And Death

Fools may pine, and sots may swill,
Cynics gibe, and prophets rail,
Moralists may scourge and drill,
Preachers prose, and fainthearts quail.
Let them whine, or threat, or wail!
Till the touch of Circumstance
Down to darkness sink the scale,
Fate's a fiddler, Life's a dance.

What if skies be wan and chill?
What if winds be harsh and stale?
Presently the east will thrill,

by William Ernest Henley

And the sad and shrunken sail
Bellying with a kindly gale,
Bear you sunwards, while your chance
Sends you back the hopeful hail: -
'Fate's a fiddler, Life's a dance.'

Idle shot or coming bill,
Hapless love or broken bail,
Gulp it (never chew your pill!)
And if Burgundy should fail,
Try the humbler pot of ail!
Over all is heaven's expanse.
Gold's to find among the shale,
Fate's a fiddler, Life's a dance.

Double Ballade on the Nothingness of Things

The big teetotum twirls,
And epochs wax and wane
As chance subsides or swirls;
But of the loss and gain
The sum is always plain.
Read on the mighty pall,
The weed of funeral
That covers praise and blame,

A Selection of Poems

The -isms and the -anities,
Magnificence and shame:--
"O Vanity of Vanities!"

The Fates are subtle girls!
They give us chaff for grain.
And Time, the Thunderer, hurls,
Like bolted death, disdain
At all that heart and brain
Conceive, or great or small,
Upon this earthly ball.
Would you be knight and dame?
Or woo the sweet humanities?
Or illustrate a name?
O Vanity of Vanities!

We sound the sea for pearls,
Or drown them in a drain;
We flute it with the merles,
Or tug and sweat and strain;
We grovel, or we reign;
We saunter, or we brawl;
We search the stars for Fame,
Or sink her subterranities;
The legend's still the same:--
"O Vanity of Vanities!"

by William Ernest Henley

Here at the wine one birls,
There some one clanks a chain.
The flag that this man furls
That man to float is fain.
Pleasure gives place to pain:
These in the kennel crawl,
While others take the wall.
She has a glorious aim,
He lives for the inanities.
What come of every claim?
O Vanity of Vanities!

Alike are clods and earls.
For sot, and seer, and swain,
For emperors and for churls,
For antidote and bane,
There is but one refrain:
But one for king and thrall,
For David and for Saul,
For fleet of foot and lame,
For pieties and profanities,
The picture and the frame:--
"O Vanity of Vanities!"

Life is a smoke that curls--

Curls in a flickering skein,
That winds and whisks and whirls,
A figment thin and vain,
Into the vast Inane.
One end for hut and hall!
One end for cell and stall!
Burned in one common flame
Are wisdoms and insanities.
For this alone we came:--
"O Vanity of Vanities!"

Envoy
Prince, pride must have a fall.
What is the worth of all
Your state's supreme urbanities?
Bad at the best's the game.
Well might the Sage exclaim:--
"O Vanity of Vanities!"

Easy is the Triolet

Easy is the Triolet,
If you really learn to make it!
Once a neat refrain you get,
Easy is the Triolet.

by William Ernest Henley

As you see! I pay my debt
With another rhyme, Deuce take it,
Easy is the Triolet,
If you really learn to make it!

England, My England

WHAT have I done for you,
   England, my England?
What is there I would not do,
   England, my own?
With your glorious eyes austere,
As the Lord were walking near,
Whispering terrible things and dear
   As the Song on your bugles blown,
   England--
   Round the world on your bugles blown!

Where shall the watchful sun,
   England, my England,
Match the master-work you've done,
   England, my own?
When shall he rejoice agen
Such a breed of mighty men
As come forward, one to ten,

To the Song on your bugles blown,
   England--
   Down the years on your bugles blown?

Ever the faith endures,
   England, my England:--
'Take and break us: we are yours,
   England, my own!
Life is good, and joy runs high
Between English earth and sky:
Death is death; but we shall die
   To the Song on your bugles blown,
   England--
   To the stars on your bugles blown!'

They call you proud and hard,
   England, my England:
You with worlds to watch and ward,
   England, my own!
You whose mail'd hand keeps the keys
Of such teeming destinies,
You could know nor dread nor ease
   Were the Song on your bugles blown,
   England,
   Round the Pit on your bugles blown!

by William Ernest Henley

Mother of Ships whose might,
   England, my England,
Is the fierce old Sea's delight,
   England, my own,
Chosen daughter of the Lord,
Spouse-in-Chief of the ancient Sword,
There 's the menace of the Word
   In the Song on your bugles blown,
   England--
   Out of heaven on your bugles blown!

Enter Patient

The morning mists still haunt the stony street;
The northern summer air is shrill and cold;
And lo, the Hospital, grey, quiet, old,
Where Life and Death like friendly chafferers meet.
Thro' the loud spaciousness and draughty gloom
A small, strange child-so aged yet so young! -
Her little arm besplinted and beslung,
Precedes me gravely to the waiting-room.
I limp behind, my confidence all gone.
The grey-haired soldier-porter waves me on,
And on I crawl, and still my spirits fail:
A tragic meanness seems so to environ

These corridors and stairs of stone and iron,
Cold, naked, clean-half-workhouse and half-jail.

Envoy--To Charles Baxter

Do you remember
That afternoon--that Sunday afternoon! -
When, as the kirks were ringing in,
And the grey city teemed
With Sabbath feelings and aspects,
LEWIS--our LEWIS then,
Now the whole world's--and you,
Young, yet in shape most like an elder, came,
Laden with BALZACS
(Big, yellow books, quite impudently French),
The first of many times
To that transformed back-kitchen where I lay
So long, so many centuries -
Or years is it!--ago?

Dear CHARLES, since then
We have been friends, LEWIS and you and I,
(How good it sounds, 'LEWIS and you and I!'):
Such friends, I like to think,
That in us three, LEWIS and me and you,

by William Ernest Henley

Is something of that gallant dream
Which old DUMAS--the generous, the humane,
The seven-and-seventy times to be forgiven! -
Dreamed for a blessing to the race,
The immortal Musketeers.

Our ATHOS rests--the wise, the kind,
The liberal and august, his fault atoned,
Rests in the crowded yard
There at the west of Princes Street. We three -
You, I, and LEWIS!--still afoot,
Are still together, and our lives,
In chime so long, may keep
(God bless the thought!)
Unjangled till the end.

Epilogue

These, to you now, O, more than ever now -
Now that the Ancient Enemy
Has passed, and we, we two that are one, have seen
A piece of perfect Life
Turn to so ravishing a shape of Death
The Arch-Discomforter might well have smiled
In pity and pride,

Even as he bore his lovely and innocent spoil
From those home-kingdoms he left desolate!

Poor windlestraws
On the great, sullen, roaring pool of Time
And Chance and Change, I know!
But they are yours, as I am, till we attain
That end for which me make, we two that are one:
A little, exquisite Ghost
Between us, smiling with the serenest eyes
Seen in this world, and calling, calling still
In that clear voice whose infinite subtleties
Of sweetness, thrilling back across the grave,
Break the poor heart to hear: -
'Come, Dadsie, come!
Mama, how long--how long!'

Etching

Two and thirty is the ploughman.
He's a man of gallant inches,
And his hair is close and curly,
And his beard;
But his face is wan and sunken,
And his eyes are large and brilliant,

by William Ernest Henley

And his shoulder-blades are sharp,
And his knees.

He is weak of wits, religious,
Full of sentiment and yearning,
Gentle, faded–with a cough
And a snore.
When his wife (who was a widow,
And is many years his elder)
Fails to write, and that is always,
He desponds.

Let his melancholy wander,
And he'll tell you pretty stories
Of the women that have wooed him
Long ago;
Or he'll sing of bonnie lasses
Keeping sheep among the heather,
With a crackling, hackling click
In his voice.

Fill A Glass With Golden Wine

Fill a glass with golden wine,
And the while your lips are wet

Set your perfume unto mine,
And forget.
Every kiss we take and give
Leaves us less of life to live.

Yet again! Your whim and mine
In a happy while have met.
All your sweets to me resign,
Nor regret
That we press with every breath,
Sighed or singing, nearer death.

Fresh From His Fastnesses

Fresh from his fastnesses
Wholesome and spacious,
The North Wind, the mad huntsman,
Halloas on his white hounds
Over the grey, roaring
Reaches and ridges,
The forest of ocean,
The chace of the world.
Hark to the peal
Of the pack in full cry,
As he thongs them before him,

by William Ernest Henley

Swarming voluminous,
Weltering, wide-wallowing,
Till in a ruining
Chaos of energy,
Hurled on their quarry,
They crash into foam!

Old Indefatigable,
Time's right-hand man, the sea
Laughs as in joy
From his millions of wrinkles:
Laughs that his destiny,
Great with the greatness
Of triumphing order,
Shows as a dwarf
By the strength of his heart
And the might of his hands.

Master of masters,
O maker of heroes,
Thunder the brave,
Irresistible message:-
'Life is worth Living
Through every grain of it,
From the foundations

To the last edge
Of the cornerstone, death.'

Friends.... Old Friends......

Friends... old friends...
One sees how it ends.
A woman looks
Or a man lies,
And the pleasant brooks
And the quiet skies,
Ruined with brawling
And caterwauling,
Enchant no more
As they did before,
And so it ends
With friends.

Friends... old friends...
And what if it ends?
Shall we dare to shirk
What we live to learn?
It has done its work,
It has served its turn;
And, forgive and forget

by William Ernest Henley

Or hanker and fret,
We can be no more
As we were before.
When it ends, it ends
With friends.

Friends… old friends…
So it breaks, so it ends.
There let it rest!
It has fought and won,
And is still the best
That either has done.
Each as he stands
The work of its hands
Which shall be more
As he was before?…
What is it ends
With friends?

From A Window In Princes Street

Above the Crags that fade and gloom
Starts the bare knee of Arthur's Seat;
Ridged high against the evening bloom,
The Old Town rises, street on street;

With lamps bejewelled, straight ahead,
Like rampired walls the houses lean,
All spired and domed and turreted,
Sheer to the valley's darkling green;
Ranged in mysterious disarray,
The Castle, menacing and austere,
Looms through the lingering last of day;
And in the silver dusk you hear,
Reverberated from crag and scar,
Bold bugles blowing points of war.

From The Break The Nightingale

From the brake the Nightingale
Sings exulting to the Rose;
Though he sees her waxing pale
In her passionate repose,
While she triumphs waxing frail,
Fading even while she glows;
Though he knows
How it goes -
Knows of last year's Nightingale
Dead with last year's Rose.

Wise the enamoured Nightingale,

by William Ernest Henley

Wise the well-beloved Rose!
Love and life shall still prevail,
Nor the silence at the close
Break the magic of the tale
In the telling, though it shows -
Who but knows
How it goes! -
Life a last year's Nightingale,
Love a last year's Rose.

Grave

St. Margaret's bells,
Quiring their innocent, old-world canticles,
Sing in the storied air,
All rosy-and-golden, as with memories
Of woods at evensong, and sands and seas
Disconsolate for that the night is nigh.
O, the low, lingering lights! The large last gleam
(Hark! how those brazen choristers cry and call!)
Touching these solemn ancientries, and there,
The silent River ranging tide-mark high
And the callow, grey-faced Hospital,
With the strange glimmer and glamour of a dream!
The Sabbath peace is in the slumbrous trees,

And from the wistful, the fast-widowing sky
(Hark! how those plangent comforters call and cry!)
Falls as in August plots late roseleaves fall.
The sober Sabbath stir -
Leisurely voices, desultory feet! -
Comes from the dry, dust-coloured street,
Where in their summer frocks the girls go by,
And sweethearts lean and loiter and confer,
Just as they did an hundred years ago,
Just as an hundred years to come they will:-
When you and I, Dear Love, lie lost and low,
And sweet-throats none our welkin shall fulfil,
Nor any sunset fade serene and slow;
But, being dead, we shall not grieve to die.

Gull In An Aery Morrice

Gulls in an aery morrice
Gleam and vanish and gleam . . .
The full sea, sleepily basking,
Dreams under skies of dream.

Gulls in an aery morrice
Circle and swoop and close . . .
Fuller and ever fuller

by William Ernest Henley

The rose of the morning blows.

Gulls, in an aery morrice
Frolicking, float and fade . . .
O, the way of a bird in the sunshine,
The way of a man with a maid!

Here They Trysted, And Here They Strayed

Here they trysted, here they strayed,
In the leafage dewy and boon,
Many a man and many a maid,
And the morn was merry June.
'Death is fleet, Life is sweet,'
Sang the blackbird in the may;
And the hour with flying feet,
While they dreamed, was yesterday.

Many a maid and many a man
Found the leafage close and boon;
Many a destiny began -
O, the morn was merry June!
Dead and gone, dead and gone,
(Hark the blackbird in the may!),
Life and Death went hurrying on,

Cheek on cheek--and where were they?

Dust on dust engendering dust
In the leafage fresh and boon,
Man and maid fulfil their trust -
Still the morn turns merry June.
Mother Life, Father Death
(O, the blackbird in the may!),
Each the other's breath for breath,
Fleet the times of the world away.

House-Surgeon

Exceeding tall, but built so well his height
Half-disappears in flow of chest and limb;
Moustache and whisker trooper-like in trim;
Frank-faced, frank-eyed, frank-hearted; always bright
And always punctual-morning, noon, and night;
Bland as a Jesuit, sober as a hymn;
Humorous, and yet without a touch of whim;
Gentle and amiable, yet full of fight.
His piety, though fresh and true in strain,
Has not yet whitewashed up his common mood
To the dead blank of his particular Schism.
Sweet, unaggressive, tolerant, most humane,

by William Ernest Henley

Wild artists like his kindly elderhood,
And cultivate his mild Philistinism.

I am the Reaper

I am the Reaper.
All things with heedful hook
Silent I gather.
Pale roses touched with the spring,
Tall corn in summer,
Fruits rich with autumn, and frail winter blossoms—
Reaping, still reaping—
All things with heedful hook
Timely I gather.

I am the Sower.
All the unbodied life
Runs through my seed-sheet.
Atom with atom wed,
Each quickening the other,
Fall through my hands, ever changing, still changeless.
Ceaselessly sowing,
Life, incorruptible life,
Flows from my seed-sheet.

Maker and breaker,
I am the ebb and the flood,
Here and Hereafter,
Sped through the tangle and coil
Of infinite nature,
Viewless and soundless I fashion all being.
Taker and giver,
I am the womb and the grave,
The Now and the Ever

I Gave My Heart To A Woman

I gave my heart to a woman –
I gave it her, branch and root.
She bruised, she wrung, she tortured,
She cast it under foot.

Under her feet she cast it,
She trampled it where it fell,
She broke it all to pieces,
And each was a clot of hell.

There in the rain and the sunshine
They lay and smouldered long;

by William Ernest Henley

And each, when again she viewed them,
Had turned to a living song.

I. M. R. T. Hamilton Bruce (1846-1899)

Out of the night that covers me,
Black as the Pit from pole to pole,
I thank whatever gods may be
For my unconquerable soul.
In the fell clutch of circumstance
I have not winced nor cried aloud.
Under the bludgeonings of chance
My head is bloody, but unbowed.
Beyond this place of wrath and tears
Looms but the Horror of the shade,
And yet the menace of the years
Finds, and shall find, me unafraid.
It matters not how strait the gate,
How charged with punishments the scroll,
I am the master of my fate:
I am the captain of my soul.

A Selection of Poems

If I Were King

If I were king, my pipe should be premier.
The skies of time and chance are seldom clear,
We would inform them all with bland blue weather.
Delight alone would need to shed a tear,
For dream and deed should war no more together.

Art should aspire, yet ugliness be dear;
Beauty, the shaft, should speed with wit for feather;
And love, sweet love, should never fall to sere,
If I were king.

But politics should find no harbour near;
The Philistine should fear to slip his tether;
Tobacco should be duty free, and beer;
In fact, in room of this, the age of leather,
An age of gold all radiant should appear,
If I were king.

If It Should Come To Be

If it should come to be,
This proof of you and me,
This type and sign

by William Ernest Henley

Of hours that smiled and shone,
And yet seemed dead and gone
As old-world wine:

Of Them Within the Gate
Ask we no richer fate,
No boon above,
For girl child or for boy,
My gift of life and joy,
Your gift of love.

In Fisherrow

A hard north-easter fifty winters long
Has bronzed and shrivelled sere her face and neck;
Her locks are wild and grey, her teeth a wreck;
Her foot is vast, her bowed leg spare and strong.
A wide blue cloak, a squat and sturdy throng
Of curt blue coats, a mutch without a speck,
A white vest broidered black, her person deck,
Nor seems their picked, stern, old-world quaintness wrong.
Her great creel forehead-slung, she wanders nigh,
Easing the heavy strap with gnarled, brown fingers,
The spirit of traffic watchful in her eye,

Ever and anon imploring you to buy,
As looking down the street she onward lingers,
Reproachful, with a strange and doleful cry.

In Rotten Row

In Rotten Row a cigarette
I sat and smoked, with no regret
For all the tumult that had been.
The distances were still and green,
And streaked with shadows cool and wet.

Two sweethearts on a bench were set,
Two birds among the boughs were met;
So love and song were heard and seen
In Rotten Row.

A horse or two there was to fret
The soundless sand; but work and debt,
Fair flowers and falling leaves between,
While clocks are chiming clear and keen,
A man may very well forget
In Rotten Row.

by William Ernest Henley

In The Dials

To GARRYOWEN upon an organ ground
Two girls are jigging. Riotously they trip,
With eyes aflame, quick bosoms, hand on hip,
As in the tumult of a witches' round.
Youngsters and youngsters round them prance and bound.
Two solemn babes twirl ponderously, and skip.
The artist's teeth gleam from his bearded lip.
High from the kennel howls a tortured hound.
The music reels and hurtles, and the night
Is full of stinks and cries; a naphtha-light
Flares from a barrow; battered and obtused
With vices, wrinkles, life and work and rags,
Each with her inch of clay, two loitering hags
Look on dispassionate--critical--something 'mused.

In The Placid Summer Midnight

In the placid summer midnight,
Under the drowsy sky,
I seem to hear in the stillness
The moths go glimmering by.

A Selection of Poems

One by one from the windows
The lights have all been sped.
Never a blind looks conscious -
The street is asleep in bed!

But I come where a living casement
Laughs luminous and wide;
I hear the song of a piano
Break in a sparkling tide;

And I feel, in the waltz that frolics
And warbles swift and clear,
A sudden sense of shelter
And friendliness and cheer . . .

A sense of tinkling glasses,
Of love and laughter and light -
The piano stops, and the window
Stares blank out into the night.

The blind goes out, and I wander
To the old, unfriendly sea,
The lonelier for the memory
That walks like a ghost with me.

by William Ernest Henley

In The Waste Hour

In the waste hour
Between to-day and yesterday
We watched, while on my arm -
Living flesh of her flesh, bone of her bone -
Dabbled in sweat the sacred head
Lay uncomplaining, still, contemptuous, strange:
Till the dear face turned dead,
And to a sound of lamentation
The good, heroic soul with all its wealth -
Its sixty years of love and sacrifice,
Suffering and passionate faith--was reabsorbed
In the inexorable Peace,
And life was changed to us for evermore.

Was nothing left of her but tears
Like blood-drops from the heart?
Nought save remorse
For duty unfulfilled, justice undone,
And charity ignored? Nothing but love,
Forgiveness, reconcilement, where in truth,
But for this passing
Into the unimaginable abyss
These things had never been?

Nay, there were we,
Her five strong sons!
To her Death came--the great Deliverer came! -
As equal comes to equal, throne to throne.
She was a mother of men.

The stars shine as of old. The unchanging River,
Bent on his errand of immortal law,
Works his appointed way
To the immemorial sea.
And the brave truth comes overwhelmingly home:-
That she in us yet works and shines,
Lives and fulfils herself,
Unending as the river and the stars.

Dearest, live on
In such an immortality
As we thy sons,
Born of thy body and nursed
At those wild, faithful breasts,
Can give--of generous thoughts,
And honourable words, and deeds
That make men half in love with fate!
Live on, O brave and true,
In us thy children, in ours whose life is thine -
Our best and theirs! What is that best but thee -

by William Ernest Henley

Thee, and thy gift to us, to pass
Like light along the infinite of space
To the immitigable end?

Between the river and the stars,
O royal and radiant soul,
Thou dost return, thine influences return
Upon thy children as in life, and death
Turns stingless! What is Death
But Life in act? How should the Unteeming Grave
Be victor over thee,
Mother, a mother of men?

In The Year That's Come and Gone

In the year that's come and gone, love, his flying feather
Stooping slowly, gave us heart, and bade us walk together.
In the year that's coming on, though many a troth be broken,
We at least will not forget aught that love hath spoken.

In the year that's come and gone, dear, we wove a

tether
All of gracious words and thoughts, binding two together.
In the year that's coming on with its wealth of roses
We shall weave it stronger, yet, ere the circle closes.

In the year that's come and gone, in the golden weather,
Sweet, my sweet, we swore to keep the watch of life together.
In the year that's coming on, rich in joy and sorrow,
We shall light our lamp, and wait life's mysterious morrow.

Interior

The gaunt brown walls
Look infinite in their decent meanness.
There is nothing of home in the noisy kettle,
The fulsome fire.

The atmosphere
Suggests the trail of a ghostly druggist.
Dressings and lint on the long, lean table -
Whom are they for?

by William Ernest Henley

The patients yawn,
Or lie as in training for shroud and coffin.
A nurse in the corridor scolds and wrangles.
It's grim and strange.

Far footfalls clank.
The bad burn waits with his head unbandaged.
My neighbour chokes in the clutch of chloral . . .
O, a gruesome world!

Interlude

O, the fun, the fun and frolic
That The Wind that Shakes the Barley
Scatters through a penny-whistle
Tickled with artistic fingers!

Kate the scrubber (forty summers,
Stout but sportive) treads a measure,
Grinning, in herself a ballet,
Fixed as fate upon her audience.

Stumps are shaking, crutch-supported;
Splinted fingers tap the rhythm;

And a head all helmed with plasters
Wags a measured approbation.

Of their mattress-life oblivious,
All the patients, brisk and cheerful,
Are encouraging the dancer,
And applauding the musician.

Dim the gas-lights in the output
Of so many ardent smokers,
Full of shadow lurch the corners,
And the doctor peeps and passes.

There are, maybe, some suspicions
Of an alcoholic presence . . .
'Tak' a sup of this, my wumman!' . . .
New Year comes but once a twelvemonth.

Invictus

Out of the night that covers me,
Black as the Pit from pole to pole,
I thank whatever gods may be
For my unconquerable soul.

by William Ernest Henley

In the fell clutch of circumstance
I have not winced nor cried aloud.
Under the bludgeonings of chance
My head is bloody, but unbowed.

Beyond this place of wrath and tears
Looms but the Horror of the shade,
And yet the menace of the years
Finds, and shall find, me unafraid.

It matters not how strait the gate,
How charged with punishments the scroll.
I am the master of my fate:
I am the captain of my soul.

It Came With The Threat Of A Waning Moon

It came with the threat of a waning moon
And the wail of an ebbing tide,
But many a woman has lived for less,
And many a man has died;
For life upon life took hold and passed,
Strong in a fate set free,
Out of the deep into the dark
On for the years to be.

Between the gloom of a waning moon
And the song of an ebbing tide,
Chance upon chance of love and death
Took wing for the world so wide.
O, leaf out of leaf is the way of the land,
Wave out of wave of the sea
And who shall reckon what lives may live
In the life that we bade to be?

Kate-A-Whimsies, John-A-Dream

Kate-a-Whimsies, John-a-Dream
Still debating, still delay,
And the world's a ghost that gleams –
Wavers – vanishes away!

We must live while live we can;
We should love while love we may.
Dread in women, doubt in men…
So the Infinite runs away.

by William Ernest Henley

Lady Probationer

Some three, or five, or seven, and thirty years;
A Roman nose; a dimpling double-chin;
Dark eyes and shy that, ignorant of sin,
Are yet acquainted, it would seem, with tears;
A comely shape; a slim, high-coloured hand,
Graced, rather oddly, with a signet ring;
A bashful air, becoming everything;
A well-bred silence always at command.
Her plain print gown, prim cap, and bright steel chain
Look out of place on her, and I remain
Absorbed in her, as in a pleasant mystery.
Quick, skilful, quiet, soft in speech and touch . . .
'Do you like nursing?' 'Yes, Sir, very much.'
Somehow, I rather think she has a history.

Largo E Mesto

Out of the poisonous East,
Over a continent of blight,
Like a maleficent Influence released
From the most squalid cellerage of hell,
The Wind-Fiend, the abominable-
The Hangman Wind that tortures temper and light-

A Selection of Poems

Comes slouching, sullen and obscene,
Hard on the skirts of the embittered night;
And in a cloud unclean
Of excremental humours, roused to strife
By the operation of some ruinous change,
Wherever his evil mandate run and range,
Into a dire intensity of life,
A craftsman at his bench, he settles down
To the grim job of throttling London Town.
So, by a jealous lightlessness beset
That might have oppressed the dragons of old time
Crunching and groping in the abysmal slime,
A cave of cut-throat thoughts and villainous dreams,
Hag-rid and crying with cold and dirt and wet,
The afflicted City. prone from mark to mark
In shameful occultation, seems
A nightmare labryrinthine, dim and drifting,
With wavering gulfs and antic heights, and shifting,
Rent in the stuff of a material dark,
Wherein the lamplight, scattered and sick and pale,
Shows like the leper's living blotch of bale:
Uncoiling monstrous into street on street
Paven with perils, teeming with mischance,
Where man and beast go blindfold and in dread,
Working with oaths and threats and faltering feet
Somewhither in the hideousness ahead;

by William Ernest Henley

Working through wicked airs and deadly dews
That make the laden robber grin askance
At the good places in his black romance,
And the poor, loitering harlot rather choose
Go pinched and pined to bed
Than lurk and shiver and curse her wretched way
From arch to arch, scouting some threepenny prey.
Forgot his dawns and far-flushed afterglows,
His green garlands and windy eyots forgot,
The old Father-River flows,
His watchfires cores of menace in the gloom,
As he came oozing from the Pit, and bore,
Sunk in his filthily transfigured sides,
Shoals of dishonoured dead to tumble and rot
In the squalor of the universal shore:
His voices sounding through the gruesome air
As from the Ferry where the Boat of Doom
With her blaspheming cargo reels and rides:
The while his children, the brave ships,
No more adventurous and fair,
Nor tripping it light of heel as home-bound brides,
But infamously enchanted,
Huddle together in the foul eclipse,
Or feel their course by inches desperately,
As through a tangle of alleys murder-haunted,
From sinister reach to reach out - out - to sea.

And Death the while -
Death with his well-worn, lean, professional smile,
Death in his threadbare working trim-
Comes to your bedside, unannounced and bland,
And with expert, inevitable hand
Feels at your windpipe, fingers you in the lung,
Or flicks the clot well into the labouring heart:
Thus signifying unto old and young,
However hard of mouth or wild of whim,
'Tis time - 'tis time by his ancient watch - to part
From books and women and talk and drink and art.
And you go humbly after him
To a mean suburban lodging: on the way
To what or where
Not Death, who is old and very wise, can say:
And you - how should you care
So long as, unreclaimed of hell,
The Wind-Fiend, the insufferable,
Thus vicious and thus patient, sits him down
To the black job of burking London Town?

Last Post

THE day's high work is over and done,
And these no more will need the sun:

by William Ernest Henley

Blow, you bugles of England, blow!
These are gone where all must go,
Mightily gone from the field they won.
So in the workaday wear of battle,
Touched to glory with God's own red,
Bear we our chosen to their bed!
Settle them lovingly where they fell,
In that good lap they loved so well;
And, their deliveries to the dear Lord said,
And the last desperate volleys ranged and sped,
Blow, you bugles of England, blow,
Over the camps of her beaten foe --
Blow glory and pity to the victor Mother,
Sad, O sad in her sacrificial dead!

Labour, and love, and strife, and mirth,
They gave their part in this kindly earth --
Blow, you bugles of England, blow!
That her Name as a sun among stars might glow,
Till the dusk of time, with honour and worth:
That stung by lust and the pain of battle,
The One Race ever might starkly spread,
And the One Flag eagle it overhead!
In a rapture of wrath and faith and pride,
Thus they felt it, and thus they died;
So to the Maker of homes, to the Giver of bread,

For whose dear sake their triumphing souls they shed,
Blow, you bugles of England, blow,
Though you break the heart of her beaten foe,
Glory and praise to the everlasting Mother,
Glory and peace to her lovely and faithful dead!

Let Us Be Drunk

Let us be drunk, and for a while forget,
Forget, and, ceasing even from regret,
Live without reason and despite of rhyme,
As in a dream preposterous and sublime,
Where place and hour and means for once are met.

Where is the use of effort? Love and debt
And disappointment have us in a net.
Let us break out, and taste the morning prime . . .
Let us be drunk.

In vain our little hour we strut and fret,
And mouth our wretched parts as for a bet:
We cannot please the tragicaster Time.
To gain the crystal sphere, the silver dime,
Where Sympathy sits dimpling on us yet,
Let us be drunk!

by William Ernest Henley

Life In Her Creaking Shoes

Life in her creaking shoes
Goes, and more formal grows,
A round of calls and cues:
Love blows as the wind blows.
Blows! . . . in the quiet close
As in the roaring mart,
By ways no mortal knows
Love blows into the heart.

The stars some cadence use,
Forthright the river flows,
In order fall the dews,
Love blows as the wind blows:
Blows! . . . and what reckoning shows
The courses of his chart?
A spirit that comes and goes,
Love blows into the heart.

Life Is Bitter

Life is bitter. All the faces of the years,
Young and old, are gray with travail and with tears.
Must we only wake to toil, to tire, to weep?

In the sun, among the leaves, upon the flowers,
Slumber stills to dreamy death the heavy hours ...
Let me sleep.

Riches won but mock the old, unable years;
Fame's a pearl that hides beneath a sea of tears;
Love must wither, or must live alone and weep.
In the sunshine, through the leaves, across the flowers,
While we slumber, death approaches through the hours ...
Let me sleep.

London Types:

Time, the old humourist, has a trick to-day
Of moving landmarks and of levelling down,
Till into Town the Suburbs edge their way,
And in the Suburbs you may scent the Town.
With Mount Street thus approaching Muswell Hill,
And Clapham Common marching with the Mile,
You get a Hammersmith that fills the bill,
A Hampstead with a serious sense of style.
So this fair creature, pictured in The Row,
As one of that 'gay adulterous world,' whose round
Is by the Serpentine, as well would show,

by William Ernest Henley

And might, I deem, as readily be found
On Streatham's Hill, or Wimbledon's, or where
Brixtonian kitchens lard the late-dining air.

London Types: Barmaid

Though, if you ask her name, she says 'Elise,'
Being plain Elizabeth, e'en let it pass,
And own that, if her aspirates take their ease,
She ever makes a point, in washing glass,
Handling the engine, turning taps for tots,
And countering change, and scorning what men say,
Of posing as a dove among the pots,
Nor often gives her dignity away.
Her head's a work of art, and, if her eyes
Be tired and ignorant, she has a waist;
Cheaply the Mode she shadows; and she tries
From penny novels to amend her taste;
And, having mopped the zinc for certain years,
And faced the gas, she fades and disappears.

A Selection of Poems

London Types: Beef-Eater

His beat lies knee-high through a dust of story-
A dust of terror and torture, grief and crime;
Ghosts that are England's wonder, and shame, and glory
Throng where he walks, an antic of old time;
A sense of long immedicable tears
Were ever with him, could his ears but heed;
The stern Hic Jacets of our bloodiest years
Are for his reading, had he eyes to read,
But here, where Crookback raged, and Cranmer trimmed,
And More and Strafford faced the axe's proving,
He shows that Crown the desperate Colonel nimmed,
Or simply keeps the Country Cousin moving,
Or stays such Cockney pencillers as would shame
The wall where some dead Queen hath traced her name.

London Types: Bluecoat Boy

So went our boys when Edward Sixth, the King,
Chartered Christ's Hospital, and died. And so
Full fifteen generations in a string

by William Ernest Henley

Of heirs to his bequest have had to go.
Thus Camden showed, and Barnes, and Stillingfleet,
And Richardson, that bade our Lovelace be;
Thus to his Genevieve young S. T. C.
With thousands else that, wandering up and down,
Quaint, privileged, liked and reputed well,
Made the great School a part of London Town
Patent as Paul's and vital as Bow Bell:
The old School nearing exile, day by day,
To certain clay-lands somewhere Horsham way.

London Types: Bus Driver

He's called The General from the brazen craft
And dash with which he sneaks a bit of road
And all its fares; challenged, or chafed, or chaffed,
Back-answers of the newest he'll explode;
He reins his horses with an air; he treats
With scoffing calm whatever powers there be;
He gets it straight, puts a bit on, and meets
His losses with both lip and £ s. d.;
He arrogates a special taste in short;
Is loftily grateful for a flagrant smoke;
At all the smarter housemaids winks his court,
And taps them for half-crowns; being stoney-broke,

Lives lustily; is ever on the make;
And hath, I fear, none other gods but Fake.

London Types: Drum-Major

Who says Drum-Major says a man of mould,
Shaking the meek earth with tremendous tread,
And pacing still, a triumph to behold,
Of his own spine at least two yards ahead!
Attorney, grocer, surgeon, broker, duke-
His calling may be anything, who comes
Into a room, his presence a rebuke
To the dejected, as the pipes and drums
Inspired his port!-who mounts his office stairs
As though he led great armies to the fight!
His bulk itself's pure genius, and he wears
His avoirdupois with so much fire and spright
That, though the creature stands but five feet five,
You take him for the tallest He alive.

London Types: Flower-Girl

There's never a delicate nurseling of the year
But our huge London hails it, and delights

by William Ernest Henley

To wear it on her breast or at her ear,
Her days to colour and make sweet her nights.
Crocus and daffodil and violet,
Pink, primrose, valley-lily, close-carnation,
Red rose and white rose, wall-flower, mignonette,
The daisies all-these be her recreation,
Her gaudies these! And forth from Drury Lane,
Trapesing in any of her whirl of weathers,
Her flower-girls foot it, honest and hoarse and vain,
All boot and little shawl and wilted feathers:
Of populous corners right advantage taking,
And, where they squat, endlessly posy-making.

London Types: Hawker

Far out of bounds he'd figured-in a race
Of West-End traffic pitching to his loss.
But if you'd see him in his proper place,
Making the browns for bub and grub and doss,
Go East among the merchants and their men,
And where the press in noisiest, and the tides
Of trade run highest and widest, there and then
You shall behold him, edging with equal strides
Along the kerb; hawking in either hand
Some artful nothing made of twine and tin,

Cardboard and foil and bits of rubber band:
Some penn'orth of wit-in-fact that, with a grin,
The careful City marvels at, and buys
For nurselings in the Suburbs to despise!

London Types: 'Liza

'Liza's old man's perhaps a little shady,
'Liza's old woman's prone to booze and cring;
But 'Liza deems herself a perfect lady,
And proves it in her feathers and her fringe.
For 'Liza has a bloke her heart to cheer,
With pearlies and a barrer and a jack,
So all the vegetables of the year
Are duly represented on her back.
Her boots are sacrifices to her hats,
Which knock you speechless-like a load of bricks!
Her summer velvets dazzle Wanstead Flats,
And cost, at times, a good eighteen-and-six.
Withal, outside the gay and giddy whirl,
'Liza's a stupid, straight, hard-working girl.

by William Ernest Henley

London Types: Mounted Police

Army Reserve; a worshipper of Bobs,
With whom he stripped the smock from Candahar;
Neat as his mount, that neatest among cobs;
Whenever pageants pass, or meetings are,
He moves conspicuous, vigilant, severe,
With his Light Cavalry hand and seat and look,
A living type of Order, in whose sphere
Is room for neither Hooligan nor Hook.
For in his shadow, wheresoe'er he ride,
Paces, all eye and hardihood and grip,
The dreaded Crusher, might in his every stride
And right materialized girt at his hip;
And they, that shake to see these twain go by,
Feel that the Tec, that plain-clothes Terror, is nigh.

London Types: News Boy

Take any station, pavement, circus, corner,
Where men their styles of print may call or choose,
And there-ten times more on it than Jack Horner-
There you shall find him swathed in sheets of news.
Nothing can stay the placing of his wares-
Not 'bus, nor cab, nor dray! The very Slop,

That imp of power, is powerless! Ever he dares,
And, daring, lands his public neck and crop.
Even the many-tortured London ear,
The much-enduring, loathes his Speeshul yell,
His shriek of Winnur! But his dart and leer
And poise are irresistible. Pall Mall
Joys in him, and Mile End; for his vocation
Is to purvey the stuff of conversation.

London Types: Sandwich-Man

An ill March noon; the flagstones gray with dust;
An all-round east wind volleying straws and grit;
St. Martin's Steps, where every venomous gust
Lingers to buffet, or sneap, the passing cit;
And in the gutter, squelching a rotten boot,
Draped in a wrap that, modish ten-year syne,
Partners, obscene with sweat and grease and soot,
A horrible hat, that once was just as fine;
The drunkard's mouth a-wash for something drinkable,
The drunkard's eye alert for causal toppers,
The drunkard's neck stooped to a lot scarce thinkable,
A living crawling blazoning of Hot-Coppers,

by William Ernest Henley

He trails his mildews towards a Kingdom-Come
Compact of sausage-and-mash and two-o'rum!

London Types: The Artist Muses At His Ease

The Artist muses at his ease,
Contented that his work is done,
And smiling-smiling!-as he sees
His crowd collecting, one by one.
Alas! his travail's but begun!
None, none can keep the years in line,
And what to Ninety-Eight is fun
May raise the gorge of Ninety-Nine!

London Types:Life-Guardsman

Joy of the Milliner, Envy of the Line,
Star of the Parks, jack-booted, sworded, helmed,
He sits between his holsters, solid of spine;
Nor, as it seems, though Westminster were whelmed,
With the great globe, in earthquake and eclipse,
Would he and his charger cease from mounting guard,
This Private in the Blues, nor would his lips
Move, though his gorge with throttled oaths were

charred!
He wears his inches weightily, as he wears
His old-world armours; and with his port and pride,
His sturdy graces and enormous airs,
He towers, in speech his Colonel countrified,
A triumph, waxing statelier year by year,
Of British blood, and bone, and beef, and beer.

London Voluntaries IV: Out of the Poisonous East

Out of the poisonous East,
Over a continent of blight,
Like a maleficent Influence released
From the most squalid cellerage of hell,
The Wind-Fiend, the abominable--
The Hangman Wind that tortures temper and light--
Comes slouching, sullen and obscene,
Hard on the skirts of the embittered night;
And in a cloud unclean
Of excremental humours, roused to strife
By the operation of some ruinous change,
Wherever his evil mandate run and range,
Into a dire intensity of life,
A craftsman at his bench, he settles down

by William Ernest Henley

To the grim job of throttling London Town.
So, by a jealous lightlessness beset
That might have oppressed the dragons of old time
Crunching and groping in the abysmal slime,
A cave of cut-throat thoughts and villainous dreams,
Hag-rid and crying with cold and dirt and wet,
The afflicted City. prone from mark to mark
In shameful occultation, seems
A nightmare labryrinthine, dim and drifting,
With wavering gulfs and antic heights, and shifting,
Rent in the stuff of a material dark,
Wherein the lamplight, scattered and sick and pale,
Shows like the leper's living blotch of bale:
Uncoiling monstrous into street on street
Paven with perils, teeming with mischance,
Where man and beast go blindfold and in dread,
Working with oaths and threats and faltering feet
Somewhither in the hideousness ahead;
Working through wicked airs and deadly dews
That make the laden robber grin askance
At the good places in his black romance,
And the poor, loitering harlot rather choose
Go pinched and pined to bed
Than lurk and shiver and curse her wretched way
From arch to arch, scouting some threepenny prey.
Forgot his dawns and far-flushed afterglows,

His green garlands and windy eyots forgot,
The old Father-River flows,
His watchfires cores of menace in the gloom,
As he came oozing from the Pit, and bore,
Sunk in his filthily transfigured sides,
Shoals of dishonoured dead to tumble and rot
In the squalor of the universal shore:
His voices sounding through the gruesome air
As from the Ferry where the Boat of Doom
With her blaspheming cargo reels and rides:
The while his children, the brave ships,
No more adventurous and fair,
Nor tripping it light of heel as home-bound brides,
But infamously enchanted,
Huddle together in the foul eclipse,
Or feel their course by inches desperately,
As through a tangle of alleys murder-haunted,
From sinister reach to reach out -- out -- to sea.
And Death the while --
Death with his well-worn, lean, professional smile,
Death in his threadbare working trim--
Comes to your bedside, unannounced and bland,
And with expert, inevitable hand
Feels at your windpipe, fingers you in the lung,
Or flicks the clot well into the labouring heart:
Thus signifying unto old and young,

by William Ernest Henley

However hard of mouth or wild of whim,
'Tis time -- 'tis time by his ancient watch -- to part
From books and women and talk and drink and art.
And you go humbly after him
To a mean suburban lodging: on the way
To what or where
Not Death, who is old and very wise, can say:
And you -- how should you care
So long as, unreclaimed of hell,
The Wind-Fiend, the insufferable,
Thus vicious and thus patient, sits him down
To the black job of burking London Town?

Madam Life's a Piece in Bloom

Madam Life's a piece in bloom
Death goes dogging everywhere:
She's the tenant of the room,
He's the ruffian on the stair.

You shall see her as a friend,
You shall bilk him once or twice;
But he'll trap you in the end,
And he'll stick you for her price.

With his kneebones at your chest,
And his knuckles in your throat,
You would reason -- plead -- protest!
Clutching at her petticoat;

But she's heard it all before,
Well she knows you've had your fun,
Gingerly she gains the door,
And your little job is done.

Margaritae Sorori

A LATE lark twitters from the quiet skies:
And from the west,
Where the sun, his day's work ended,
Lingers as in content,
There falls on the old, gray city
An influence luminous and serene,
A shining peace.

The smoke ascends
In a rosy-and-golden haze. The spires
Shine and are changed. In the valley
Shadows rise. The lark sings on. The sun,
Closing his benediction,

by William Ernest Henley

Sinks, and the darkening air
Thrills with a sense of the triumphing night--
Night with her train of stars
And her great gift of sleep.

So be my passing!
My task accomplish'd and the long day done,
My wages taken, and in my heart
Some late lark singing,
Let me be gather'd to the quiet west,
The sundown splendid and serene,
Death.

Midsummer Midnight Skies

Midsummer midnight skies,
Midsummer midnight influences and airs,
The shining, sensitive silver of the sea
Touched with the strange-hued blazonings of dawn;
And all so solemnly still I seem to hear
The breathing of Life and Death,
The secular Accomplices,
Renewing the visible miracle of the world.

The wistful stars

A Selection of Poems

Shine like good memories. The young morning wind
Blows full of unforgotten hours
As over a region of roses. Life and Death
Sound on--sound on . . . And the night magical,
Troubled yet comforting, thrills
As if the Enchanted Castle at the heart
Of the wood's dark wonderment
Swung wide his valves, and filled the dim sea-banks
With exquisite visitants:
Words fiery-hearted yet, dreams and desires
With living looks intolerable, regrets
Whose voice comes as the voice of an only child
Heard from the grave: shapes of a Might-Have-Been -
Beautiful, miserable, distraught -
The Law no man may baffle denied and slew.

The spell-bound ships stand as at gaze
To let the marvel by. The grey road glooms . . .
Glimmers . . . goes out . . . and there, O, there where it fades,
What grace, what glamour, what wild will,
Transfigure the shadows? Whose,
Heart of my heart, Soul of my soul, but yours?

Ghosts--ghosts--the sapphirine air
Teems with them even to the gleaming ends

by William Ernest Henley

Of the wild day-spring! Ghosts,
Everywhere--everywhere--till I and you
At last--dear love, at last! -
Are in the dreaming, even as Life and Death,
Twin-ministers of the unoriginal Will.

Music

Down the quiet eve,
Thro' my window with the sunset
Pipes to me a distant organ
Foolish ditties;

And, as when you change
Pictures in a magic lantern,
Books, beds, bottles, floor, and ceiling
Fade and vanish,

And I'm well once more . . .
August flares adust and torrid,
But my heart is full of April
Sap and sweetness.

In the quiet eve
I am loitering, longing, dreaming . . .

Dreaming, and a distant organ
Pipes me ditties.

I can see the shop,
I can smell the sprinkled pavement,
Where she serves-her chestnut chignon
Thrills my senses!

O, the sight and scent,
Wistful eve and perfumed pavement!
In the distance pipes an organ . . .
The sensation

Comes to me anew,
And my spirit for a moment
Thro' the music breathes the blessed
Airs of London.

Nocturn

At the barren heart of midnight,
When the shadow shuts and opens
As the loud flames pulse and flutter,
I can hear a cistern leaking.

by William Ernest Henley

Dripping, dropping, in a rhythm,
Rough, unequal, half-melodious,
Like the measures aped from nature
In the infancy of music;

Like the buzzing of an insect,
Still, irrational, persistent . . .
I must listen, listen, listen
In a passion of attention;

Till it taps upon my heartstrings,
And my very life goes dripping,
Dropping, dripping, drip-drip-dropping,
In the drip-drop of the cistern.

Not To The Staring Day

Not to the staring Day,
For all the importunate questionings he pursues
In his big, violent voice,
Shall those mild things of bulk and multitude,
The Trees--God's sentinels
Over His gift of live, life-giving air,
Yield of their huge, unutterable selves.
Midsummer-manifold, each one

A Selection of Poems

Voluminous, a labyrinth of life,
They keep their greenest musings, and the dim dreams
That haunt their leafier privacies,
Dissembled, baffling the random gapeseed still
With blank full-faces, or the innocent guile
Of laughter flickering back from shine to shade,
And disappearances of homing birds,
And frolicsome freaks
Of little boughs that frisk with little boughs.

But at the word
Of the ancient, sacerdotal Night,
Night of the many secrets, whose effect -
Transfiguring, hierophantic, dread -
Themselves alone may fully apprehend,
They tremble and are changed.
In each, the uncouth individual soul
Looms forth and glooms
Essential, and, their bodily presences
Touched with inordinate significance,
Wearing the darkness like the livery
Of some mysterious and tremendous guild,
They brood--they menace--they appal;
Or the anguish of prophecy tears them, and they wring
Wild hands of warning in the face

by William Ernest Henley

Of some inevitable advance of the doom;
Or, each to the other bending, beckoning, signing
As in some monstrous market-place,
They pass the news, these Gossips of the Prime,
In that old speech their forefathers
Learned on the lawns of Eden, ere they heard
The troubled voice of Eve
Naming the wondering folk of Paradise.

Your sense is sealed, or you should hear them tell
The tale of their dim life, with all
Its compost of experience: how the Sun
Spreads them their daily feast,
Sumptuous, of light, firing them as with wine;
Of the old Moon's fitful solicitude
And those mild messages the Stars
Descend in silver silences and dews;
Or what the sweet-breathing West,
Wanton with wading in the swirl of the wheat,
Said, and their leafage laughed;
And how the wet-winged Angel of the Rain
Came whispering . . . whispering; and the gifts of the Year -
The sting of the stirring sap
Under the wizardry of the young-eyed Spring,
Their summer amplitudes of pomp,

Their rich autumnal melancholy, and the shrill,
Embittered housewifery
Of the lean Winter: all such things,
And with them all the goodness of the Master,
Whose right hand blesses with increase and life,
Whose left hand honours with decay and death.

Thus under the constraint of Night
These gross and simple creatures,
Each in his scores of rings, which rings are years,
A servant of the Will!
And God, the Craftsman, as He walks
The floor of His workshop, hearkens, full of cheer
In thus accomplishing
The aims of His miraculous artistry.

O Gather Me the Rose

O gather me the rose, the rose,
While yet in flower we find it,
For summer smiles, but summer goes,
And winter waits behind it.

For with the dream foregone, foregone,
The deed foreborn forever,

by William Ernest Henley

The worm Regret will canker on,
And time will turn him never.

So were it well to love, my love,
And cheat of any laughter
The fate beneath us, and above,
The dark before and after.

The myrtle and the rose, the rose,
The sunshine and the swallow,
The dream that comes, the wish that goes
The memories that follow!

O, Falmouth Is a Fine Town

O Falmouth is a fine town with ships in the bay,
And I wish from my heart it's there I was to-day;
I wish from my heart I was far away from here,
Sitting in my parlor and talking to my dear.
For it's home, dearie home-it's home I want to be.
Our topsails are hoisted, and we'll away to sea.
O the oak and the ash and the bonnie birken tree,
They're all growing green in the old countrie.

In Baltimore a-walking a lady I did meet

With her babe on her arm as she came down the street;
And I thought how I sailed, and the cradle standing ready
For the pretty little babe that has never seen its daddie.
And it's home, dearie, home,-

O, if it be a lass, she shall wear a golden ring;
And if it be a lad, he shall fight for his king;
With his dirk and his hat and his little jacket blue
He shall walk the quarter-deck as his daddie used to do.
And it's home, dearie, home-

O, there's a wind a-blowing, a-blowing from the west,
And that of all the winds is the one I like the best,
For it blows at our backs, and it shakes our pennon free,
And it soon will blow us home to the old countrie.
For it's home, dearie, home-it's home I want to be.
Our topsails are hoisted, and we'll away to sea.
O, the oak and the ash and the bonnie birken tree,
They're all growing green in the old countrie.

by William Ernest Henley

O, Have You Blessed, Behind The Stars

O, have you blessed, behind the stars,
The blue sheen of the skies,
When June the roses round her calls? –
Then do you know the light that falls
From her beloved eyes.

And have you felt the sense of peace
That morning meadows give? –
Then do you know the spirit of grace,
The angel abiding in her face,
Who makes it good to live.

She shines before me, hope and dream,
So fair, so still, so wise,
That winning her, I seem to won
Out of the dust and drive and din
A nook of Paradise.

O, Time And Change, They Range And Range

O, Time and Change, they range and range
From sunshine round to thunder! -

They glance and go as the great winds blow,
And the best of our dreams drive under:
For Time and Change estrange, estrange -
And, now they have looked and seen us,
O, we that were dear, we are all-too near
With the thick of the world between us.

O, Death and Time, they chime and chime
Like bells at sunset falling! -
They end the song, they right the wrong,
They set the old echoes calling:
For Death and Time bring on the prime
Of God's own chosen weather,
And we lie in the peace of the Great Release
As once in the grass together.

On The Way To Kew

On the way to Kew,
By the river old and gray,
Where in the Long Ago,
We laughed and loitered so,
I met a ghost to-day,
A ghost that told of you –
A ghost of old replies

by William Ernest Henley

And sweet, inscrutable eyes
Coming up from Richmond
As you used to do.

By the river old and gray,
The enchanted Long Ago
Murmured and smiled anew.
On the way to Kew,
March had the laugh of May,
The bare boughs looked aglow,
And old immortal words
Sang in my breast like birds,
Coming up from Richmond
As I used with you.

With the life of Long Ago
Lived my thought of you.
By the river old and gray
Flowing his appointed way
As I watched I knew
What is good to know –
Not in vain, not in vain,
Shall I look for you again
Coming up from Richmond
On the way to Kew.

A Selection of Poems

One With The Ruined Sunset

One with the ruined sunset,
The strange forsaken sands,
What is it waits, and wanders,
And signs with desparate hands?

What is it calls in the twilight -
Calls as its chance were vain?
The cry of a gull sent seaward
Or the voice of an ancient pain?

The red ghost of the sunset,
It walks them as its own,
These dreary and desolate reaches . . .
But O, that it walked alone!

Operation

You are carried in a basket,
Like a carcase from the shambles,
To the theatre, a cockpit
Where they stretch you on a table.

Then they bid you close your eyelids,

by William Ernest Henley

And they mask you with a napkin,
And the anaesthetic reaches
Hot and subtle through your being.

And you gasp and reel and shudder
In a rushing, swaying rapture,
While the voices at your elbow
Fade-receding-fainter-farther.

Li ghts about you shower and tumble,
And your blood seems crystallising -
Edged and vibrant, yet within you
Racked and hurried back and forward.

Then the lights grow fast and furious,
And you hear a noise of waters,
And you wrestle, blind and dizzy,
In an agony of effort,

Till a sudden lull accepts you,
And you sound an utter darkness . . .
And awaken . . . with a struggle . . .
On a hushed, attentive audience.

A Selection of Poems

Orientale

She's an enchanting little Israelite,
A world of hidden dimples!--Dusky-eyed,
A starry-glancing daughter of the Bride,
With hair escaped from some Arabian Night,
Her lip is red, her cheek is golden-white,
Her nose a scimitar; and, set aside
The bamboo hat she cocks with so much pride,
Her dress a dream of daintiness and delight.
And when she passes with the dreadful boys
And romping girls, the cockneys loud and crude,
My thought, to the Minories tied yet moved to range
The Land o' the Sun, commingles with the noise
Of magian drums and scents of sandalwood
A touch Sidonian--modern--taking--strange!

Out Of The Night That Covers Me

Out of the night that covers me,
Black as the Pit from pole to pole,
I thank whatever gods may be
For my unconquerable soul.

In the fell clutch of circumstance

by William Ernest Henley

I have not winced nor cried aloud.
Under the bludgeonings of chance
My head is bloody, but unbowed.

Beyond this place of wrath and tears
Looms but the Horror of the shade,
And yet the menace of the years
Finds, and shall find, me unafraid.

It matters not how strait the gate,
How charged with punishments the scroll.
I am the master of my fate:
I am the captain of my soul.

Over the Hills and Far Away

Where forlorn sunsets flare and fade
On desolate sea and lonely sand,
Out of the silence and the shade
What is the voice of strange command
Calling you still, as friend calls friend
With love that cannot brook delay,
To rise and follow the ways that wend
Over the hills and far away?

Hark in the city, street on street
A roaring reach of death and life,
Of vortices that clash and fleet
And ruin in appointed strife,
Hark to it calling, calling clear,
Calling until you cannot stay
From dearer things than your own most dear
Over the hills and far away.

Out of the sound of the ebb-and-flow,
Out of the sight of lamp and star,
It calls you where the good winds blow,
And the unchanging meadows are;
From faded hopes and hopes agleam,
It calls you, calls you night and day
Beyond the dark into the dream
Over the hills and far away.

Pastoral

It's the Spring.
Earth has conceived, and her bosom,
Teeming with summer, is glad.

Vistas of change and adventure,

by William Ernest Henley

Thro' the green land
The grey roads go beckoning and winding,
Peopled with wains, and melodious
With harness-bells jangling:
Jangling and twangling rough rhythms
To the slow march of the stately, great horses
Whistled and shouted along.

White fleets of cloud,
Argosies heavy with fruitfulness,
Sail the blue peacefully. Green flame the hedgerows.
Blackbirds are bugling, and white in wet winds
Sway the tall poplars.
Pageants of colour and fragrance,
Pass the sweet meadows, and viewless
Walks the mild spirit of May,
Visibly blessing the world.

O, the brilliance of blossoming orchards!
O, the savour and thrill of the woods,
When their leafage is stirred
By the flight of the Angel of Rain!
Loud lows the steer; in the fallows
Rooks are alert; and the brooks
Gurgle and tinkle and trill. Thro' the gloamings,
Under the rare, shy stars,

Boy and girl wander,
Dreaming in darkness and dew.

It's the Spring.
A sprightliness feeble and squalid
Wakes in the ward, and I sicken,
Impotent, winter at heart.

Praise The Generous Gods

Praise the generous gods for giving
In a world of wrath and strife,
With a little time for living,
Unto all the joy of life.

At whatever source we drink it,
Art or life or faith or wine,
In whatever terms we think it,
It is common and divine.

Praise the high gods, for in giving
This for man, and this alone,
They have made his chance for living
Shine the equal of their own.

by William Ernest Henley

Pro Rege Nostro

WHAT have I done for you,
England, my England?
What is there I would not do,
England, my own?
With your glorious eyes austere,
As the Lord were walking near,
Whispering terrible things and dear
As the Song on your bugles blown, England --
Round the world on your bugles blown!

Where shall the watchful Sun,
England, my England,
Match the master-work you've done,
England, my own?
When shall he rejoice again
Such a breed of mighty men
As come forward, one to ten,
To the Song on your bugles blown, England --
Down the years on your bugles blown?

Ever the faith endures,
England, my England: --
'Take and break us: we are yours,
England, my own!

A Selection of Poems

Life is good, and joy runs high
Between English earth and sky:
Death is death; but we shall die
To the Song on your bugles blown, England --
To the stars on your bugles blown!'

They call you proud and hard,
England, my England:
You with worlds to watch and ward,
England, my own!
You whose mailed hand keeps the keys
Of such teeming destinies,
You could know nor dread nor ease,
Were the Song on your bugles blown, England --
Round the Pit on your bugles blown!

Mother of Ships whose might,
England, my England,
Is the fierce old Sea's delight,
England, my own,
Chosen daughter of the Lord,
Spouse-in-Chief of the ancient Sword,
There's the menace of the Word
In the Song of your bugles blown, England --
Out of heaven on your bugles blown!

by William Ernest Henley

Prologue

Something is dead . . .
The grace of sunset solitudes, the march
Of the solitary moon, the pomp and power
Of round on round of shining soldier-stars
Patrolling space, the bounties of the sun -
Sovran, tremendous, unimaginable -
The multitudinous friendliness of the sea,
Possess no more--no more.

Something is dead . . .
The Autumn rain-rot deeper and wider soaks
And spreads, the burden of Winter heavier weighs,
His melancholy close and closer yet
Cleaves, and those incantations of the Spring
That made the heart a centre of miracles
Grow formal, and the wonder-working bours
Arise no more--no more.

Something is dead . . .
'Tis time to creep in close about the fire
And tell grey tales of what we were, and dream
Old dreams and faded, and as we may rejoice
In the young life that round us leaps and laughs,
A fountain in the sunshine, in the pride

Of God's best gift that to us twain returns,
Dear Heart, no more--no more.

Romance

'Talk of pluck!' pursued the Sailor,
Set at euchre on his elbow,
'I was on the wharf at Charleston,
Just ashore from off the runner.

'It was grey and dirty weather,
And I heard a drum go rolling,
Rub-a-dubbing in the distance,
Awful dour-like and defiant.

'In and out among the cotton,
Mud, and chains, and stores, and anchors,
Tramped a squad of battered scarecrows -
Poor old Dixie's bottom dollar!

'Some had shoes, but all had rifles,
Them that wasn't bald was beardless,
And the drum was rolling Dixie,
And they stepped to it like men, sir!

by William Ernest Henley

'Rags and tatters, belts and bayonets,
On they swung, the drum a-rolling,
Mum and sour. It looked like fighting,
And they meant it too, by thunder!'

Scherzando

Down through the ancient Strand
The spirit of October, mild and boon
And sauntering, takes his way
This golden end of afternoon,
As though the corn stood yellow in all the land,
And the ripe apples dropped to the harvest-moon.

Lo! the round sun, half-down the western slope -
Seen as along an unglazed telescope -
Lingers and lolls, loth to be done with day:
Gifting the long, lean, lanky street
And its abounding confluences of being
With aspects generous and bland;
Making a thousand harnesses to shine
As with new ore from some enchanted mine,
And every horse's coat so full of sheen
He looks new-tailored, and every 'bus feels clean,
And never a hansom but is worth the feeing;

And every jeweller within the pale
Offers a real Arabian Night for sale;
And even the roar
Of the strong streams of toil, that pause and pour
Eastward and westward, sounds suffused -
Seems as it were bemused
And blurred, and like the speech
Of lazy seas on a lotus-haunted beach -
With this enchanted lustrousness,
This mellow magic, that (as a man's caress
Brings back to some faded face, beloved before,
A heavenly shadow of the grace it wore
Ere the poor eyes were minded to beseech)
Old things transfigures, and you hail and bless
Their looks of long-lapsed loveliness once more:
Till Clement's, angular and cold and staid,
Gleams forth in glamour's very stuffs arrayed;
And Bride's, her aery, unsubstantial charm
Through flight on flight of springing, soaring stone
Grown flushed and warm,
Laughs into life full-mooded and fresh-blown;
And the high majesty of Paul's
Uplifts a voice of living light, and calls -
Calls to his millions to behold and see
How goodly this his London Town can be!

by William Ernest Henley

For earth and sky and air
Are golden everywhere,
And golden with a gold so suave and fine
The looking on it lifts the heart like wine.
Trafalgar Square
(The fountains volleying golden glaze)
Shines like an angel-market. High aloft
Over his couchant Lions, in a haze
Shimmering and bland and soft,
A dust of chrysoprase,
Our Sailor takes the golden gaze
Of the saluting sun, and flames superb,
As once he flamed it on his ocean round.
The dingy dreariness of the picture-place,
Turned very nearly bright,
Takes on a luminous transiency of grace,
And shows no more a scandal to the ground.
The very blind man pottering on the kerb,
Among the posies and the ostrich feathers
And the rude voices touched with all the weathers
Of the long, varying year,
Shares in the universal alms of light.
The windows, with their fleeting, flickering fires,
The height and spread of frontage shining sheer,
The quiring signs, the rejoicing roofs and spires -
'Tis El Dorado--El Dorado plain,

The Golden City! And when a girl goes by,
Look! as she turns her glancing head,
A call of gold is floated from her ear!
Golden, all golden! In a golden glory,
Long-lapsing down a golden coasted sky,
The day, not dies but, seems
Dispersed in wafts and drifts of gold, and shed
Upon a past of golden song and story
And memories of gold and golden dreams.

Scrubber

She's tall and gaunt, and in her hard, sad face
With flashes of the old fun's animation
There lowers the fixed and peevish resignation
Bred of a past where troubles came apace.
She tells me that her husband, ere he died,
Saw seven of their children pass away,
And never knew the little lass at play
Out on the green, in whom he's deified.
Her kin dispersed, her friends forgot and gone,
All simple faith her honest Irish mind,
Scolding her spoiled young saint, she labours on:
Telling her dreams, taking her patients' part,

by William Ernest Henley

Trailing her coat sometimes: and you shall find
No rougher, quainter speech, nor kinder heart.

She Saunters By The Swinging Seas

She sauntered by the swinging seas,
A jewel glittered at her ear,
And, teasing her along, the breeze
Brought many a rounded grace more near.

So passing, one with wave and beam,
She left for memory to caress
A laughing thought, a golden gleam,
A hint of hidden loveliness.

Some Starlit Garden Grey With Dew

Some starlit garden grey with dew,
Some chamber flushed with wine and fire,
What matters where, so I and you
Are worthy our desire?

Behind, a past that scolds and jeers
For ungirt loins and lamps unlit;

In front, the unmanageable years,
The trap upon the Pit;

Think on the shame of dreams for deeds,
The scandal of unnatural strife,
The slur upon immortal needs,
The treason done to life:

Arise! no more a living lie,
And with me quicken and control
Some memory that shall magnify
The universal Soul.

Space And Dread and The Dark

Space and dread and the dark -
Over a livid stretch of sky
Cloud-monsters crawling, like a funeral train
Of huge, primeval presences
Stooping beneath the weight
Of some enormous, rudimentary grief;
While in the haunting loneliness
The far sea waits and wanders with a sound
As of the trailing skirts of Destiny,
Passing unseen

by William Ernest Henley

To some immitigable end
With her grey henchman, Death.

What larve, what spectre is this
Thrilling the wilderness to life
As with the bodily shape of Fear?
What but a desperate sense,
A strong foreboding of those dim
Interminable continents, forlorn
And many-silenced, in a dusk
Inviolable utterly, and dead
As the poor dead it huddles and swarms and styes
In hugger-mugger through eternity?

Life--life--let there be life!
Better a thousand times the roaring hours
When wave and wind,
Like the Arch-Murderer in flight
From the Avenger at his heel,
Storm through the desolate fastnesses
And wild waste places of the world!

Life--give me life until the end,
That at the very top of being,
The battle-spirit shouting in my blood,
Out of the reddest hell of the fight

I may be snatched and flung
Into the everlasting lull,
The immortal, incommunicable dream.

Staff Nurse: New Style

Blue-eyed and bright of face but waning fast
Into the sere of virginal decay,
I view her as she enters, day by day,
As a sweet sunset almost overpast.
Kindly and calm, patrician to the last,
Superbly falls her gown of sober gray,
And on her chignon's elegant array
The plainest cap is somehow touched with caste.
She talks BEETHOVEN; frowns disapprobation
At BALZAC'S name, sighs it at 'poor GEORGE SAND'S';
Knows that she has exceeding pretty hands;
Speaks Latin with a right accentuation;
And gives at need (as one who understands)
Draught, counsel, diagnosis, exhortation.

by William Ernest Henley

Staff Nurse: Old Style

The greater masters of the commonplace,
REMBRANDT and good SIR WALTER-only these
Could paint her all to you: experienced ease
And antique liveliness and ponderous grace;
The sweet old roses of her sunken face;
The depth and malice of her sly, grey eyes;
The broad Scots tongue that flatters, scolds, defies;
The thick Scots wit that fells you like a mace.
These thirty years has she been nursing here,
Some of them under SYME , her hero still.
Much is she worth, and even more is made of her.
Patients and students hold her very dear.
The doctors love her, tease her, use her skill.
They say 'The Chief' himself is half-afraid of her.

Suicide

Staring corpselike at the ceiling,
See his harsh, unrazored features,
Ghastly brown against the pillow,
And his throat-so strangely bandaged!

Lack of work and lack of victuals,

A debauch of smuggled whisky,
And his children in the workhouse
Made the world so black a riddle

That he plunged for a solution;
And, although his knife was edgeless,
He was sinking fast towards one,
When they came, and found, and saved him.

Stupid now with shame and sorrow,
In the night I hear him sobbing.
But sometimes he talks a little.
He has told me all his troubles.

In his broad face, tanned and bloodless,
White and wild his eyeballs glisten;
And his smile, occult and tragic,
Yet so slavish, makes you shudder!

The Chief

His brow spreads large and placid, and his eye
Is deep and bright, with steady looks that still.
Soft lines of tranquil thought his face fulfill -
His face at once benign and proud and shy.

by William Ernest Henley

If envy scout, if ignorance deny,
His faultless patience, his unyielding will,
Beautiful gentleness and splendid skill,
Innumerable gratitudes reply.
His wise, rare smile is sweet with certainties,
And seems in all his patients to compel
Such love and faith as failure cannot quell.
We hold him for another Herakles,
Battling with custom, prejudice, disease,
As once the son of Zeus with Death and Hell.

The Full Sea Rolls And Thunders

The full sea rolls and thunders
In glory and in glee.
O, bury me not in the senseless earth
But in the living sea!

Ay, bury me where it surges
A thousand miles from shore,
And in its brotherly unrest
I'll range for evermore.

A Selection of Poems

The Gods Are Dead

The gods are dead? Perhaps they are! Who knows?
Living at least in Lempriere undeleted,
The wise, the fair, the awful, the jocose,
Are one and all. I like to think, retreated
In some still land of lilacs and the rose.

Once high they sat, and high o'er earthly shows
With sacrificial dance and song were greeted.
Once… long ago. But now, the story goes,
The gods are dead.

It must be true. The world, a world of prose,
Full-crammed with facts, in science swathed and sheeted,
Nods in a stertorous after-dinner doze!
Plangent and sad, in every wind that blows
Who will may hear the sorry words repeated: –
'The Gods are Dead!'

The Nightingale Has A Lyre Of Gold

The nightingale has a lyre of gold,
The lark's is a clarion-call,

by William Ernest Henley

And the blackbird plays but a boxwood flute,
But I love him best of all.

For his song is all of the joy of life,
And we in the mad, spring weather,
We two have listened till he sang
Our hearts and lips together.

The Past Was Goodly Once

The Past was goodly once, and yet, when all is said,
The best of it we know is that it's done and dead.

Dwindled and faded quite, perished beyond recall,
Nothing is left at last of what one time was all.

Coming back like a ghost, staring and lingering on,
Never a word it speaks but proves it dead and gone.

Duty and work and joy--these things it cannot give;
And the Present is life, and life is good to live.

Let it lie where it fell, far from the living sun,
The Past that, goodly once, is gone and dead and done.

A Selection of Poems

The Rain and the Wind

The rain and the wind, the wind and the rain --
They are with us like a disease:
They worry the heart, they work the brain,
As they shoulder and clutch at the shrieking pane,
And savage the helpless trees.

What does it profit a man to know
These tattered and tumbling skies
A million stately stars will show,
And the ruining grace of the after-glow
And the rush of the wild sunrise?

Ever the rain -- the rain and the wind!
Come, hunch with me over the fire,
Dream of the dreams that leered and grinned,
Ere the blood of the Year got chilled and thinned,
And the death came on desire!

The Sands Are Alive With Sunshine

The sands are alive with sunshine,
The bathers lounge and throng,
And out in the bay a bugle

by William Ernest Henley

Is lilting a gallant song.

The clouds go racing eastward,
The blithe wind cannot rest,
And a shard on the shingle flashes
Like the shining soul of a jest;

While children romp in the surges,
And sweethearts wander free,
And the Firth as with laughter dimples . . .
I would it were deep over me!

The Sea Is Full Of Wandering Foam

The sea is full of wandering foam,
The sky of driving cloud;
My restless thoughts among them roam . . .
The night is dark and loud.

Where are the hours that came to me
So beautiful and bright?
A wild wind shakes the wilder sea . . .
O, dark and loud's the night!

A Selection of Poems

The Shadow Of Dawn

The shadow of Dawn;
Stillness and stars and over-mastering dreams
Of Life and Death and Sleep;
Heard over gleaming flats, the old, unchanging sound
Of the old, unchanging Sea.

My soul and yours -
O, hand in hand let us fare forth, two ghosts,
Into the ghostliness,
The infinite and abounding solitudes,
Beyond--O, beyond!--beyond . . .

Here in the porch
Upon the multitudinous silences
Of the kingdoms of the grave,
We twain are you and I--two ghosts Omnipotence
Can touch no more . . . no more!

The Skies Are Strown With Stars

The skies are strown with stars,
The streets are fresh with dew
A thin moon drifts to westward,

by William Ernest Henley

The night is hushed and cheerful.
My thought is quick with you.

Near windows gleam and laugh,
And far away a train
Clanks glowing through the stillness:
A great content's in all things,
And life is not in vain.

The Song Of The Sword--To Rudyard Kipling

The Sword
Singing -
The voice of the Sword from the heart of the Sword
Clanging imperious
Forth from Time's battlements
His ancient and triumphing Song.

In the beginning,
Ere God inspired Himself
Into the clay thing
Thumbed to His image,
The vacant, the naked shell
Soon to be Man:
Thoughtful He pondered it,

A Selection of Poems

Prone there and impotent,
Fragile, inviting
Attack and discomfiture;
Then, with a smile -
As He heard in the Thunder
That laughed over Eden
The voice of the Trumpet,
The iron Beneficence,
Calling his dooms
To the Winds of the world -
Stooping, He drew
On the sand with His finger
A shape for a sign
Of his way to the eyes
That in wonder should waken,
For a proof of His will
To the breaking intelligence.
That was the birth of me:
I am the Sword.

Bleak and lean, grey and cruel,
Short-hilted, long shafted,
I froze into steel;
And the blood of my elder,
His hand on the hafts of me,
Sprang like a wave

by William Ernest Henley

In the wind, as the sense
Of his strength grew to ecstasy;
Glowed like a coal
In the throat of the furnace;
As he knew me and named me
The War-Thing, the Comrade,
Father of honour
And giver of kingship,
The fame-smith, the song-master,
Bringer of women
On fire at his hands
For the pride of fulfilment,
PRIEST (saith the Lord)
OF HIS MARRIAGE WITH VICTORY
Ho! then, the Trumpet,
Handmaid of heroes,
Calling the peers
To the place of espousals!
Ho! then, the splendour
And glare of my ministry,
Clothing the earth
With a livery of lightnings!
Ho! then, the music
Of battles in onset,
And ruining armours,
And God's gift returning

In fury to God!
Thrilling and keen
As the song of the winter stars,
Ho! then, the sound
Of my voice, the implacable
Angel of Destiny! -
I am the Sword.

Heroes, my children,
Follow, O, follow me!
Follow, exulting
In the great light that breaks
From the sacred Companionship!
Thrust through the fatuous,
Thrust through the fungous brood,
Spawned in my shadow
And gross with my gift!
Thrust through, and hearken
O, hark, to the Trumpet,
The Virgin of Battles,
Calling, still calling you
Into the Presence,
Sons of the Judgment,
Pure wafts of the Will!
Edged to annihilate,
Hilted with government,

by William Ernest Henley

Follow, O, follow me,
Till the waste places
All the grey globe over
Ooze, as the honeycomb
Drips, with the sweetness
Distilled of my strength,
And, teeming in peace
Through the wrath of my coming,
They give back in beauty
The dread and the anguish
They had of me visitant!
Follow, O follow, then,
Heroes, my harvesters!
Where the tall grain is ripe
Thrust in your sickles!
Stripped and adust
In a stubble of empire,
Scything and binding
The full sheaves of sovranty:
Thus, O, thus gloriously,
Shall you fulfil yourselves!
Thus, O, thus mightily,
Show yourselves sons of mine -
Yea, and win grace of me:
I am the Sword!

A Selection of Poems

I am the feast-maker:
Hark, through a noise
Of the screaming of eagles,
Hark how the Trumpet,
The mistress of mistresses,
Calls, silver-throated
And stern, where the tables
Are spread, and the meal
Of the Lord is in hand!
Driving the darkness,
Even as the banners
And spears of the Morning;
Sifting the nations,
The slag from the metal,
The waste and the weak
From the fit and the strong;
Fighting the brute,
The abysmal Fecundity;
Checking the gross,
Multitudinous blunders,
The groping, the purblind
Excesses in service
Of the Womb universal,
The absolute drudge;
Firing the charactry
Carved on the World,

by William Ernest Henley

The miraculous gem
In the seal-ring that burns
On the hand of the Master -
Yea! and authority
Flames through the dim,
Unappeasable Grisliness
Prone down the nethermost
Chasms of the Void! -
Clear singing, clean slicing;
Sweet spoken, soft finishing;
Making death beautiful,
Life but a coin
To be staked in the pastime
Whose playing is more
Than the transfer of being;
Arch-anarch, chief builder,
Prince and evangelist,
I am the Will of God:
I am the Sword.

The Sword
Singing -
The voice of the Sword from the heart of the Sword
Clanging majestical,
As from the starry-staired

Courts of the primal Supremacy,
His high, irresistible song.

The Spirit Of Wine

The Spirit of Wine
Sang in my glass, and I listened
With love to his odorous music,
His flushed and magnificent song.

- 'I am health, I am heart, I am life!
For I give for the asking
The fire of my father, the Sun,
And the strength of my mother, the Earth.
Inspiration in essence,
I am wisdom and wit to the wise,
His visible muse to the poet,
The soul of desire to the lover,
The genius of laughter to all.

'Come, lean on me, ye that are weary!
Rise, ye faint-hearted and doubting!
Haste, ye that lag by the way!
I am Pride, the consoler;
Valour and Hope are my henchmen;

by William Ernest Henley

I am the Angel of Rest.

'I am life, I am wealth, I am fame:
For I captain an army
Of shining and generous dreams;
And mine, too, all mine, are the keys
Of that secret spiritual shrine,
Where, his work-a-day soul put by,
Shut in with his saint of saints -
With his radiant and conquering self -
Man worships, and talks, and is glad.

'Come, sit with me, ye that are lovely,
Ye that are paid with disdain,
Ye that are chained and would soar!
I am beauty and love;
I am friendship, the comforter;
I am that which forgives and forgets.' -

The Spirit of Wine
Sang in my heart, and I triumphed
In the savour and scent of his music,
His magnetic and mastering song.

A Selection of Poems

The Spring, My Dear

The spring, my dear,
Is no longer spring.
Does the blackbird sing
What he sang last year?
Are the skies the old
Immemorial blue?
Or am I, or are you,
Grown cold?

Though life be change,
It is hard to bear
When the old sweet air
Sounds forced and strange.
To be out of tune,
Plain You and I . . .
It were better to die,
And soon!

The Surges Gushed And Sounded

The surges gushed and sounded,
The blue was the blue of June,
And low above the brightening east

by William Ernest Henley

Floated a shred of moon.

The woods were black and solemn,
The night winds large and free,
And in your thought a blessing seemed
To fall on land and sea.

The Wan Sun Westers, Faint And Slow

The wan sun westers, faint and slow;
The eastern distance glimmers gray;
An eerie haze comes creeping low
Across the little, lonely bay;
And from the sky-line far away
About the quiet heaven are spread
Mysterious hints of dying day,
Thin, delicate dreams of green and red.

And weak, reluctant surges lap
And rustle round and down the strand.
No other sound . . . If it should hap,
The ship that sails from fairy-land!
The silken shrouds with spells are manned,
The hull is magically scrolled,
The squat mast lives, and in the sand

The gold prow-griffin claws a hold.

It steals to seaward silently;
Strange fish-folk follow thro' the gloom;
Great wings flap overhead; I see
The Castle of the Drowsy Doom
Vague thro' the changeless twilight loom,
Enchanted, hushed. And ever there
She slumbers in eternal bloom,
Her cushions hid with golden hair.

The Ways Are Green

The ways are green with the gladdening sheen
Of the young year's fairest daughter.
O, the shadows that fleet o'er the springing wheat!
O, the magic of running water!
The spirit of spring is in every thing,
The banners of spring are streaming,
We march to a tune from the fifes of June,
And life's a dream worth dreaming.

It's all very well to sit and spell
At the lesson there's no gainsaying;
But what the deuce are wont and use

by William Ernest Henley

When the whole mad world's a-maying?
When the meadow glows, and the orchard snows,
And the air's with love-motes teeming,
When fancies break, and the senses wake,
O, life's a dream worth dreaming!

What Nature has writ with her lusty wit
Is worded so wisely and kindly
That whoever has dipped in her manuscript
Must up and follow her blindly.
Now the summer prime is her blithest rhyme
In the being and the seeming,
And they that have heard the overword
Know life's a dream worth dreaming.

The Ways Of Death Are Soothing And Serene

The ways of Death are soothing and serene,
And all the words of Death are grave and sweet.
From camp and church, the fireside and the street,
She beckons forth – and strife and song have been.

A summer night descending cool and green
And dark on daytime's dust and stress and heat,
The ways of death are soothing and serene,

And all the words of Death are grave and sweet.

O, glad and sorrowful, with triumphant mien
And radiant faces, look upon and greet
This last of all your lovers, and to meet
The kiss, the Comforter's, your spirit lean ....
The ways of Death are soothing and serene.

The West A Glimmering Lake Of Light

The West a glimmering lake of light,
A dream of pearly weather,
The first of stars is burning white -
The star we watch together.
Is April dead? The unresting year
Will shape us our September,
And April's work is done, my dear -
Do you not remember?

O gracious eve! O happy star,
Still-flashing, glowing, sinking! -
Who lives of lovers near or far
So glad as I in thinking?
The gallant world is warm and green,
For May fulfils November.

by William Ernest Henley

When lights and leaves and loves have been,
Sweet, will you remember?

O star benignant and serene,
I take the good to-morrow,
That fills from verge to verge my dream,
With all its joy and sorrow!
The old, sweet spell is unforgot
That turns to June December;
And, tho' the world remembered not,
Love, we would remember.

There Is A Wheel Inside My Head

There is a wheel inside my head
Of wantonness and wine,
An old, cracked fiddle is begging without,
But the wind with scents of the sea is fed,
And the sun seems glad to shine.

The sun and the wind are akin to you,
As you are akin to June.
But the fiddle! . . . It giggles and twitters about,
And, love and laughter! who gave him the cue? -
He's playing your favourite tune.

A Selection of Poems

There's a Regret

There's a regret
So grinding, so immitigably sad,
Remorse thereby feels tolerant, even glad. ...
Do you not know it yet?

For deeds undone
Rnakle and snarl and hunger for their due,
Till there seems naught so despicable as you
In all the grin o' the sun.

Like an old shoe
The sea spurns and the land abhors, you lie
About the beach of Time, till by and by
Death, that derides you too --

Death, as he goes
His ragman's round, espies you, where you stray,
With half-an-eye, and kicks you out of his way
And then -- and then, who knows

But the kind Grave
Turns on you, and you feel the convict Worm,
In that black bridewell working out his term,
Hanker and grope and crave?

by William Ernest Henley

"Poor fool that might --
That might, yet would not, dared not, let this be,
Think of it, here and thus made over to me
In the implacable night!"

And writhing, fain
And like a triumphing lover, he shall take,
His fill where no high memory lives to make
His obscene victory vain.

Thick Is The Darkness

Thick is the darkness -
Sunward, O, sunward!
Rough is the highway -
Onward, still onward!

Dawn harbours surely
East of the shadows.
Facing us somewhere
Spread the sweet meadows.

Upward and forward!
Time will restore us:

Light is above us,
Rest is before us.

Time And The Earth

Time and the Earth -
The old Father and Mother -
Their teeming accomplished,
Their purpose fulfilled,
Close with a smile
For a moment of kindness,
Ere for the winter
They settle to sleep.

Failing yet gracious,
Slow pacing, soon homing,
A patriarch that strolls
Through the tents of his children,
The Sun, as he journeys
His round on the lower
Ascents of the blue,
Washes the roofs
And the hillsides with clarity;
Charms the dark pools
Till they break into pictures;

by William Ernest Henley

Scatters magnificent
Alms to the beggar trees;
Touches the mist-folk,
That crowd to his escort,
Into translucencies
Radiant and ravishing:
As with the visible
Spirit of Summer
Gloriously vaporised,
Visioned in gold!

Love, though the fallen leaf
Mark, and the fleeting light
And the loud, loitering
Footfall of darkness
Sign to the heart
Of the passage of destiny,
Here is the ghost
Of a summer that lived for us,
Here is a promise
Of summers to be.

A Selection of Poems

To Me At My Fifth-Floor Window

To me at my fifth-floor window
The chimney-pots in rows
Are sets of pipes pandean
For every wind that blows;

And the smoke that whirls and eddies
In a thousand times and keys
Is really a visible music
Set to my reveries.

O monstrous pipes, melodious
With fitful tune and dream,
The clouds are your only audience,
Her thought is your only theme!

To My Mother

Chiming a dream by the way
With ocean's rapture and roar,
I met a maiden to-day
Walking alone on the shore:
Walking in maiden wise,
Modest and kind and fair,

by William Ernest Henley

The freshness of spring in her eyes
And the fullness of spring in her hair.

Cloud-shadow and scudding sun-burst
Where swift on the floor of the sea,
And a mad wind was romping its worst,
But what was their magic to me?
Or the charm of the midsummer skies?
I only saw she was there,
A dream of the sea in her eyes
And the kiss of the sea in her hair.

I watch her vanish in space;
She came where I walked no more;
But something was passed from her grace
To the spell of the wave and the shore;
And now as the glad stars rise,
She comes to me, rosy and rare,
The delight of the wind in her eyes
And the hand of the wind in her hair.

To My Wife

Take, dear, my little sheaf of songs,
For, old or new,

All that is good in them belongs
Only to you;

And, singing as when all was young,
They will recall
Those others, lived but left unsung –
The best of all

To: W A

Or ever the knightly years were gone
With the old world to the grave,
I was a King in Babylon
And you were a Christian Slave.

I saw, I took, I cast you by,
I bent and broke your pride.
You loved me well, or I heard them lie,
But your longing was denied.
Surely I knew that by and by
You cursed your gods and died.

And a myriad suns have set and shone
Since then upon the grave
Decreed by the King in Babylon

by William Ernest Henley

To her that had been his Slave.

The pride I trampled is now my scathe,
For it tramples me again.
The old resentment lasts like death,
For you love, yet you refrain.
I break my heart on your hard unfaith,
And I break my heart in vain.

Yet not for an hour do I wish undone
The deed beyond the grave,
When I was a King in Babylon
And you were a Virgin Slave.

Tree, Old Tree Of The Triple Crook

Tree, Old Tree of the Triple Crook
And the rope of the Black Election,
'Tis the faith of the Fool that a race you rule
Can never achieve perfection:
So 'It's O, for the time of the new Sublime
And the better than human way,
When the Rat (poor beast) shall come to his own
And the Wolf shall have his day!'

A Selection of Poems

For Tree, Old Tree of the Triple Beam
And the power of provocation,
You have cockered the Brute with your dreadful fruit
Till your fruit is mere stupration:
And 'It's how should we rise to be pure and wise,
And how can we choose but fall,
So long as the Hangman makes us dread,
And the Noose floats free for all?'

So Tree, Old Tree of the Triple Coign
And the trick there's no recalling,
They will haggle and hew till they hack you through
And at last they lay you sprawling:
When 'Hey! for the hour of the race in flower
And the long good-bye to sin!'
And for the lack the fires of Hell gone out
Of the fuel to keep them in!'

But Tree, Old Tree of the Triple Bough
And the ghastly Dreams that tend you,
Your growth began with the life of Man,
And only his death can end you.
They may tug in line at your hempen twine,
They may flourish with axe and saw;
But your taproot drinks of the Sacred Springs
In the living rock of Law.

by William Ernest Henley

And Tree, Old Tree of the Triple Fork,
When the spent sun reels and blunders
Down a welkin lit with the flare of the Pit
As it seethes in spate and thunders,
Stern on the glare of the tortured air
Your lines august shall gloom,
And your master-beam be the last thing whelmed
In the ruining roar of Doom.

Trees And The Menace Of Night

Trees and the menace of night;
Then a long, lonely, leaden mere
Backed by a desolate fell,
As by a spectral battlement; and then,
Low-brooding, interpenetrating all,
A vast, gray, listless, inexpressive sky,
So beggared, so incredibly bereft
Of starlight and the song of racing worlds,
It might have bellied down upon the Void
Where as in terror Light was beginning to be.

Hist! In the trees fulfilled of night
(Night and the wretchedness of the sky)

A Selection of Poems

Is it the hurry of the rain?
Or the noise of a drive of the Dead,
Streaming before the irresistible Will
Through the strange dusk of this, the Debateable Land
Between their place and ours?

Like the forgetfulness
Of the work-a-day world made visible,
A mist falls from the melancholy sky.
A messenger from some lost and loving soul,
Hopeless, far wandered, dazed
Here in the provinces of life,
A great white moth fades miserably past.

Thro' the trees in the strange dead night,
Under the vast dead sky,
Forgetting and forgot, a drift of Dead
Sets to the mystic mere, the phantom fell,
And the unimagined vastitudes beyond.

Unconquerable

Put of the night that covers me,
Black as the Pit from pole to pole,

by William Ernest Henley

I thank whatever gods may be
For my unconquerable soul.

In the full clutch of circumstances
I have not winced nor cried aloud.
Under the bludgeonings of chance
My head is bloody, but unbowed.

Beyond this place of wrath and tears
Looms but the Horror of the shade,
And yet the menace of the years
Finds, and shall find, me unafraid.

It matters not how straight the gate,
How charged with punishments the scroll,
I am the master of my fate:
I am the captain of my soul.

Under A Stagnant Sky

Under a stagnant sky,
Gloom out of gloom uncoiling into gloom,
The River, jaded and forlorn,
Welters and wanders wearily--wretchedly--on;
Yet in and out among the ribs

Of the old skeleton bridge, as in the piles
Of some dead lake-built city, full of skulls,
Worm-worn, rat-riddled, mouldy with memories,
Lingers to babble to a broken tune
(Once, O, the unvoiced music of my heart!)
So melancholy a soliloquy
It sounds as it might tell
The secret of the unending grief-in-grain,
The terror of Time and Change and Death,
That wastes this floating, transitory world.

What of the incantation
That forced the huddled shapes on yonder shore
To take and wear the night
Like a material majesty?
That touched the shafts of wavering fire
About this miserable welter and wash -
(River, O River of Journeys, River of Dreams!) -
Into long, shining signals from the panes
Of an enchanted pleasure-house,
Where life and life might live life lost in life
For ever and evermore?

O Death! O Change! O Time!
Without you, O, the insuperable eyes

by William Ernest Henley

Of these poor Might-Have-Beens,
These fatuous, ineffectual Yesterdays!

Vigil

Lived on one's back,
In the long hours of repose,
Life is a practical nightmare -
Hideous asleep or awake.

Shoulders and loins
Ache-- -!
Ache, and the mattress,
Run into boulders and hummocks,
Glows like a kiln, while the bedclothes -
Tumbling, importunate, daft -
Ramble and roll, and the gas,
Screwed to its lowermost,
An inevitable atom of light,
Haunts, and a stertorous sleeper
Snores me to hate and despair.

All the old time
Surges malignant before me;
Old voices, old kisses, old songs

Blossom derisive about me;
While the new days
Pass me in endless procession:
A pageant of shadows
Silently, leeringly wending
On . . . and still on . . . still on!

Far in the stillness a cat
Languishes loudly. A cinder
Falls, and the shadows
Lurch to the leap of the flame. The next man to me
Turns with a moan; and the snorer,
The drug like a rope at his throat,
Gasps, gurgles, snorts himself free, as the night-nurse,
Noiseless and strange,
Her bull's eye half-lanterned in apron,
(Whispering me, 'Are ye no sleepin' yet?'),
Passes, list-slippered and peering,
Round . . . and is gone.

Sleep comes at last -
Sleep full of dreams and misgivings -
Broken with brutal and sordid
Voices and sounds that impose on me,
Ere I can wake to it,
The unnatural, intolerable day.

by William Ernest Henley

Villanelle

A dainty thing's the Villanelle.
Sly, musical, a jewel in rhyme,
It serves its purpose passing well.

A double-clappered silver bell
That must be made to clink in chime,
A dainty thing's the Villanelle;

And if you wish to flute a spell,
Or ask a meeting 'neath the lime,
It serves its purpose passing well.

You must not ask of it the swell
Of organs grandiose and sublime-
A dainty thing's the Villanelle;

And, filled with sweetness, as a shell
Is filled with sound, and launched in time,
It serves its purpose passing well.

Still fair to see and good to smell
As in the quaintness of its prime,
A dainty thing's the Villanelle,
It serves its purpose passing well.

A Selection of Poems

Villon's Straight Tip to All Cross Coves

"Tout aux tavernes et aux filles."
Suppose you screeve? or go cheap-jack?
Or fake the broads? or fig a nag?
Or thimble-rig? or knap a yack?
Or pitch a snide? or smash a rag?
Suppose you duff? or nose and lag?
Or get the straight, and land your pot?
How do you melt the multy swag?
Booze and the blowens cop the lot.
Fiddle, or fence, or mace, or mack;
Or moskeneer, or flash the drag;
Dead-lurk a crib, or do a crack;
Pad with a slang, or chuck a fag;
Bonnet, or tout, or mump and gag;
Rattle the tats, or mark the spot;
You can not bank a single stag;
Booze and the blowens cop the lot.
Suppose you try a different tack,
And on the square you flash your flag?
At penny-a-lining make your whack,
Or with the mummers mug and gag?
For nix, for nix the dibbs you bag!
At any graft, no matter what,
Your merry goblins soon stravag:

by William Ernest Henley

Booze and the blowens cop the lot.
THE MORAL

It's up the spout and Charley Wag
With wipes and tickers and what not.
Until the squeezer nips your scrag,
Booze and the blowens cop the lot.

Visitor

Her little face is like a walnut shell
With wrinkling lines; her soft, white hair adorns
Her withered brows in quaint, straight curls, like horns;
And all about her clings an old, sweet smell.
Prim is her gown and quakerlike her shawl.
Well might her bonnets have been born on her.
Can you conceive a Fairy Godmother
The subject of a strong religious call?
In snow or shine, from bed to bed she runs,
All twinkling smiles and texts and pious tales,
Her mittened hands, that ever give or pray,
Bearing a sheaf of tracts, a bag of buns:
A wee old maid that sweeps the Bridegroom's way,
Strong in a cheerful trust that never fails.

Waiting

A square, squat room (a cellar on promotion),
Drab to the soul, drab to the very daylight;
Plasters astray in unnatural-looking tinware;
Scissors and lint and apothecary's jars.

Here, on a bench a skeleton would writhe from,
Angry and sore, I wait to be admitted:
Wait till my heart is lead upon my stomach,
While at their ease two dressers do their chores.

One has a probe-it feels to me a crowbar.
A small boy sniffs and shudders after bluestone.
A poor old tramp explains his poor old ulcers.
Life is (I think) a blunder and a shame.

We Are The Choice Of The Will

We are the Choice of the Will: God, when He gave the word
That called us into line, set in our hand a sword;

Set us a sword to wield none else could lift and draw,
And bade us forth to the sound of the trumpet of the

by William Ernest Henley

Law.

East and west and north, wherever the battle grew,
As men to a feast we fared, the work of the Will to do.

Bent upon vast beginnings, bidding anarchy cease -
(Had we hacked it to the Pit, we had left it a place of peace!) -

Marching, building, sailing, pillar of cloud or fire,
Sons of the Will, we fought the fight of the Will, our sire.

Road was never so rough that we left its purpose dark;
Stark was ever the sea, but our ships were yet more stark;

We tracked the winds of the world to the steps of their very
thrones;
The secret parts of the world were salted with our bones;

Till now the name of names, England, the name of might,
Flames from the austral fires to the bounds of the

boreal night;

And the call of her morning drum goes in a girdle of sound,
Like the voice of the sun in song, the great globe round and round;

And the shadow of her flag, when it shouts to the mother-breeze,
Floats from shore to shore of the universal seas;

And the loneliest death is fair with a memory of her flowers,
And the end of the road to Hell with the sense of her dews and
showers!

Who says that we shall pass, or the fame of us fade and die,
While the living stars fulfil their round in the living sky?

For the sire lives in his sons, and they pay their father's debt,
And the Lion has left a whelp wherever his claw was set;

by William Ernest Henley

And the Lion in his whelps, his whelps that none shall brave,
Is but less strong than Time and the great, all-whelming Grave.

We Flash Across The Level

We flash across the level.
We thunder thro' the bridges.
We bicker down the cuttings.
We sway along the ridges.

A rush of streaming hedges,
Of jostling lights and shadows,
Of hurtling, hurrying stations,
Of racing woods and meadows.

We charge the tunnels headlong -
The blackness roars and shatters.
We crash between embankments -
The open spins and scatters.

We shake off the miles like water,
We might carry a royal ransom;

And I think of her waiting, waiting,
And long for a common hansom.

We Shall Surely Die

We shall surely die:
Must we needs grow old?
Grow old and cold,
And we know not why?

O, the By-and-By,
And the tale that's told!
We shall surely die:
Must we needs grow old?

Grow old and sigh,
Grudge and withhold,
Resent and scold?...
Not you and I?
We shall surely die!

by William Ernest Henley

We'll go No More A-Roving

We'll go no more a-roving by the light of the moon.
November glooms are barren beside the dusk of June.
The summer flowers are faded, the summer thoughts are sere.
We'll go no more a-roving, lest worse befall, my dear.

We'll go no more a-roving by the light of the moon.
The song we sang rings hollow, and heavy runs the tune.
Glad ways and words remembered would shame the wretched year.
We'll go no more a-roving, nor dream we did, my dear.

We'll go no more a-roving by the light of the moon.
If yet we walk together, we need not shun the noon.
No sweet thing left to savour, no sad thing left to fear,
We'll go no more a-roving, but weep at home, my dear.

A Selection of Poems

What Have I Done For You

What have I done for you,
England, my England?
What is there I would not do,
England, my own?
With your glorious eyes austere,
As the Lord were walking near,
Whispering terrible things and dear
As the Song on your bugles blown,
England -
Round the world on your bugles blown!

Where shall the watchful Sun,
England, my England,
Match the master-work you've done,
England, my own?
When shall he rejoice agen
Such a breed of mighty men
As come forward, one to ten,
To the Song on your bugles blown,
England -
Down the years on your bugles blown?

Ever the faith endures,
England, my England:-

by William Ernest Henley

'Take and break us: we are yours,
'England, my own!
'Life is good, and joy runs high
'Between English earth and sky:
'Death is death; but we shall die
'To the Song on your bugles blown,
'England -
'To the stars on your bugles blown!

They call you proud and hard,
England, my England:
You with worlds to watch and ward,
England, my own!
You whose mailed hand keeps the keys
Of such teeming destinies
You could know nor dread nor ease
Were the Song on your bugles blown,
England,
Round the Pit on your bugles blown!

Mother of Ships whose might,
England, my England,
Is the fierce old Sea's delight,
England, my own,
Chosen daughter of the Lord,
Spouse-in-Chief of the ancient sword,

A Selection of Poems

There's the menace of the Word
In the Song on your bugles blown,
England -
Out of heaven on your bugles blown!

What Is To Come

What is to come we know not. But we know
That what has been was good--was good to show,
Better to hide, and best of all to bear.
We are the masters of the days that were:
We have lived, we have loved, we have suffered . . . even so.

Shall we not take the ebb who had the flow?
Life was our friend. Now, if it be our foe -
Dear, though it spoil and break us!--need we care
What is to come?

Let the great winds their worst and wildest blow,
Or the gold weather round us mellow slow:
We have fulfilled ourselves, and we can dare
And we can conquer, though we may not share
In the rich quiet of the afterglow
What is to come.

by William Ernest Henley

When The Wind Storms By With A Shout

When the wind storms by with a shout, and the stern sea-caves
Rejoice in the tramp and the roar of onsetting waves,
Then, then, it comes home to the heart that the top of life
Is the passion that burns the blood in the act of strife -
Till you pity the dead down there in their quiet graves.

But to drowse with the fen behind and the fog before,
When the rain-rot spreads and a tame sea mumbles the shore,
Not to adventure, none to fight, no right and no wrong,
Sons of the Sword heart-sick for a stave of your sire's old song -
O, you envy the blessed death that can live no more!

When You Are Old

When you are old, and I am passed away –
Passed, and your face, your golden face is gray –
I think, what'er the end, this dream of mine,

Comforting you, a friendly star will shine
Down the dim slope where you still stumble and stray.
So may it be: that so dead yesterday,
Not sad-eyed ghost but generous and gay,
May serve your memories like almighty wine,
When you are old!

Dear Heart, it shall be so. Under the sway
Of death the past's enormous disarray
Lies hushed and dark. Yet though there come no sign,
Live on well pleased: immortal and divine
Love shall still tend you, as God's angels may,
When you are old.

When You Wake In Your Crib

When you wake in your crib,
You, an inch of experience -
Vaulted about
With the wonder of darkness;
Wailing and striving
To reach from your feebleness
Something you feel
Will be good to and cherish you,
Something you know

by William Ernest Henley

And can rest upon blindly:
O, then a hand
(Your mother's, your mother's!)
By the fall of its fingers
All knowledge, all power to you,
Out of the dreary,
Discouraging strangenesses
Comes to and masters you,
Takes you, and lovingly
Woos you and soothes you
Back, as you cling to it,
Back to some comforting
Corner of sleep.

So you wake in your bed,
Having lived, having loved;
But the shadows are there,
And the world and its kingdoms
Incredibly faded;
And you group through the Terror
Above you and under
For the light, for the warmth,
The assurance of life;
But the blasts are ice-born,
And your heart is nigh burst
With the weight of the gloom

And the stress of your strangled
And desperate endeavour:
Sudden a hand -
Mother, O Mother! -
God at His best to you,
Out of the roaring,
Impossible silences,
Falls on and urges you,
Mightily, tenderly,
Forth, as you clutch at it,
Forth to the infinite
Peace of the Grave.

Where Forlorn Sunsets Flare And Fade

Where forlorn sunsets flare and fade
On desolate sea and lonely sand,
Out of the silence and the shade
What is the voice of strange command
Calling you still, as friend calls friend
With love that cannot brook delay
To rise and follow the ways that wend
Over the hills and far away?

Hark in the city, street on street

by William Ernest Henley

A roaring reach of death and life,
Of vortices that clash and fleet
And ruin in appointed strife,
Hark to it calling, calling clear,
Calling until you cannot stay
From dearer things than your own most dear
Over the hills and far away?

Out of the sound of the ebb-and-flow,
Out of the sight of the lamp and star,
It calls you where the good winds blow,
And the unchanging meadows are;
From faded hopes and hopes agleam,
It calls you, calls you night and day
Beyond the dark into the dream
Over the hills and far away.

While The West Is Paling

While the west is paling
Starshine is begun.
While the dusk is failing
Glimmers up the sun.

So, till darkness cover

A Selection of Poems

Life's retreating gleam,
Lover follows lover,
Dream succeeds to dream.

Stoop to my endeavour,
O my love, and be
Only and for ever
Sun and stars to me.

Why, My Heart, Do We Love Her So?

Why, my heart, do we love her so?
(Geraldine, Geraldine!)
Why does the great sea ebb and flow? -
Why does the round world spin?
Geraldine, Geraldine,
Bid me my life renew:
What is it worth unless I win,
Love--love and you?

Why, my heart, when we speak her name
(Geraldine, Geraldine!)
Throbs the word like a flinging flame? -
Why does the Spring begin?
Geraldine, Geraldine,

by William Ernest Henley

Bid me indeed to be:
Open your heart, and take us in,
Love--love and me.

You Played And Sang A Snatch Of Song

You played and sang a snatch of song,
A song that all-too well we knew;
But whither had flown the ancient wrong;
And was it really I and you?
O, since the end of life's to live
And pay in pence the common debt,
What should it cost us to forgive
Whose daily task is to forget?

You babbled in the well-known voice -
Not new, not new the words you said.
You touched me off that famous poise,
That old effect, of neck and head.
Dear, was it really you and I?
In truth the riddle's ill to read,
So many are the deaths we die
Before we can be dead indeed.

A Selection of Poems

Your Heart Has Trembled To My Tongue

Your heart has trembled to my tongue,
Your hands in mine have lain,
Your thought to me has leaned and clung,
Again and yet again,
My dear,
Again and yet again.

Now die the dream, or come the wife,
The past is not in vain,
For wholly as it was your life
Can never be again,
My dear,
Can never be again.

www.ingramcontent.com/pod-product-compliance
Lightning Source LLC
Chambersburg PA
CBHW021148160426
43194CB00007B/732